Trust in the Lord with all your heart and lean not on your own understanding.Acknowledge him in all your ways,and he will make your paths straight.Don't be wise in your own opinion. Fear the Lord and depart from evil;For it will be medicine for your body,and refreshment for your bones.

Proverbs 3:5-8

In relationships between parents and their children, problems often arise from poor communication. This is why Proverbs offers a wise recommendation: "The wise man speaks little, and the intelligent man knows how to control himself…" (Proverbs 17:27).

Poor communication forms the foundation that hinders the resolution of other conflicts between both parties. It can manipulate the relationship, leading to oppositional attitudes, coexistence issues, lack of respect, violence, and more. As both a father and a son, I encountered two choices in life: #1 Continue a toxic pattern that would harm the people I love, or #2 Adjust my actions and renew my understanding to protect my loved ones. I chose the latter, and this decision allowed me to embrace what I now regard as my greatest treasure: "My Family."

In this book, Daniel addresses essential points for achieving healthy communication and building relationships free from resentment. It is more than just a book; it serves as a guide filled with valuable tools, fully supported by the word of God, which is perfect and leads us to all truth.

—James Pérez
Author of the books:
"It is Written,"
"The 3 Places Where Satan Wants to Curse You",
"60 Minutes with God."

When I read the early chapters of this book, I was thrilled to discover practical tools aimed at enhancing relationships between parents and children. We all know that no parents or children are perfect; that's precisely why knowledge is so important. By absorbing it, we can act with wisdom and prudence in raising our children, ultimately breaking the toxic cycles that have plagued our family connections.

Daniel writes not only from the perspective of a son but also as a father. He presents insights from two crucial angles, which are essential for building healthy relationships. His approach emphasizes that family dynamics should not be about fighting each other but rather about wielding swords against the true enemy.

—Samara Pérez
Author of the books:
"Declarations of Life for Women,"
"60 Minutes with God"

How many times can we apologize for lacking the education, information, or resources to improve our lives as parents? In this book, you will discover invaluable insights that will inspire you to become a better father or mother and challenge you to grow as a person!

I have known Daniel since he was eight years old, and I've witnessed the hand of God work in his life over the years. You can truly feel the inspiration of God as you read the pages of this book, which address themes that are deeply relevant to our times. Every parent should have this book in their hands!
Invest in your own life so that you can also invest in the lives of your children. Our children are a precious gift from God, and it is our duty to disciple and guide them to become better than we are. "Fists of Swords" is an eye-opener filled with valuable information and sound advice for the entire family.

—M.ED,Victor B.Calderon
Professor at Seattle Central College
Author of the Book:"#Cheer-up."

When I began reading the first paragraphs, I was immediately drawn to the theme of the book. As parents, if we could only grasp the emotional backpacks we place on our children! While we're taught not to pick at the scabs of our physical wounds to aid in healing, no one educates us on how to heal the emotional wounds of the soul, as highlighted in 3 John 1:2: "Beloved, I wish you to prosper in everything, just as your soul heals."

Many of these emotional backpacks do not belong to us; they

are inherited from our parents or grandparents. Studies from the University of Chile have shown that multi-problem families and those living in poverty across 16 Latin American countries pass down disorganization, dysfunctional dynamics, and poor communication across up to three or four generations. The lack of parental attachment and secure bonds with children and primary caregivers contributes to this issue. Among the many challenges a child faces in the world, the fear of abandonment stands out prominently.

What happens when the fear of abandonment gets carried from one emotional suitcase to another? Many have experienced feelings of abandonment from conception, through maternal care, kindergarten, primary school, and into adulthood. These experiences often lead to behaviors such as codependency, rooted in the wound of abandonment. Communication is another significant issue; we complain about its absence or inadequacy without realizing that we're always communicating, whether verbally or non-verbally.

To enhance communication within a couple or family, it's essential to raise awareness about what happens during the communication process, including the subconscious or automatic communication patterns we may unknowingly exhibit.

This book is an invaluable resource for every family—an excellent tool to educate, correct, teach, and guide. Thank you, Daniel Becerra, for this essential work!

—Psychologist. María Isabel Olmos Ojeda
Expert in Domestic Violence
Thanatologist
Family & Couple Therapy

Fists To Swords
By Daniel J.Becerra

Contact with Author:becerradaniel22@gmail.com

Editing and correction by Daniel J.Becerra
Cover Design by: Daniel J.Becerra.
ISBN: 9798227047717

Imprint: Independently published

I Dedicate this book:
To God who shows his love,mercy and kindness
towards my life every day.

To my wife Wendy,for loving me and supporting
me in all my projects.

To my daughter Aylani for being
the Engine of my Life

To every child and father who wants to
have an excellent family relationship

FISTS TO SWORDS

HOW TO RESOLVE DIFFICULT FAMILY PROBLEMS

DANIEL J. BECERRA

Table of Contents

BREAKING PARADIGMS

Changing culture and lifestyle is not easy; in fact, it's one of the most difficult challenges for individuals with deep-rooted habits developed over time. Those who are parents often mirror the family dynamics they experienced as children, adopting various reactions—both positive and negative. The influence of parents is powerful and lasting, establishing what we call "Engendered Habits" or traditional cultures.

These traditions become entrenched because of the absence of change. For instance, fathers who exhibit sexist behavior towards mothers may instill feelings of insecurity and trauma in their children through their discouraging words and actions. As Jesus said, "If any of you want to be my follower, you must abandon your own way of life, take up your cross daily, and follow me" (Luke 9:23 NLT). This call to abandon our old ways is essential for aspiring to be better people—seeking to please God through our lives and making a meaningful impact on others.

Change begins with a conscious decision to start anew, which often involves letting go of harmful traditions and customs, as well as the wounds of the past. It requires breaking patterns that negatively affect families and moving beyond ideologies that hinder progress. Many generations have suffered due to outdated beliefs, leading too many parents to replicate toxic patterns in raising their children.

Moreover, the notion that parents are exempt from apologizing to their children for past mistakes needs to be challenged. This mindset can entrap children of well-meaning Christian parents in cycles of addiction or disillusionment, as they witness a disconnect between their parents' beliefs and actions.

This book aims to illuminate your perspective regarding family management. Change demands bravery and honesty, as true healing and salvation are only possible through confronting the root causes of problems. Jesus embodies the path to improvement; through Him, transformation is attainable. Breaking paradigms isn't optional; it is imperative to embrace a changed mindset to understand God's loving direction.

Consider this book your guide towards spiritual and emotional healing—a tool designed to help you foster a healthier relationship with your children. Instead of engaging in trivial conflicts, it encourages the development of integrity, compassion, and faith.

By breaking free from limitations that have held your family back, you can begin a journey shaped by positive actions and words. It's fundamental to reflect on your past mistakes while committing to responsible actions moving forward.

This book will offer strategies for effective communication with your children—without resorting to hurtful language or actions. Allow God to lead you through this transformation. Your children deserve a parent who strives to be the best version of themselves. Let go of any outdated habits or beliefs that do not but the eventual rewards bring peace and fulfillment to your life.

Remember, it's never too late to start anew. Today presents an opportunity to reshape your existence and become a better person. Don't lose hope—your sacrifices and commitment will lead to tranquility and a brighter future.
serve your growth. Change demands effort,

—DANIEL J. BECERRA.

READING GUIDE

Dear Parent,
It is my hope that you can develop your abilities by reading this book. To do this, I want to recommend the most effective way for you to understand, analyze, and fully develop the steps in this book. Jesus told the parable of the Sower, who went out to scatter seeds in the field. This parable illustrates how different environments affect growth and understanding:

The seeds that fell on the road were quickly devoured by birds. Those in shallow soil, with rocks beneath, soon withered under the heat of the sun as they lacked deep roots. The seeds that fell among thorns grew but were choked and produced no grain. However, the seeds that fell on fertile soil yielded a harvest that was thirty, sixty, and even a hundred times larger than what had been sown.

In this book, I encourage you to be like the fertile soil that receives the word, puts it into practice, and produces numerous fruits that will make you a better Christian, a better parent, and ultimately, a true follower of Jesus. Before diving in, make sure you thoroughly read the introduction, the prologue, and all the initial content. This groundwork will help you understand the language, the purpose, and the destination of this writing. It's not just about reading for knowledge; it's about transformation.

This book is designed to help you identify and correct your mistakes as you read. It encourages you to change habits and thoughts that you may have previously considered correct, helping you recalibrate your approach to parenting and relationships. Embrace this journey with an open heart, and you will find the guidance you need to grow and thrive.
Wishing you all the best on this enriching path!

I leave you some recommendations so that you can understand the book and make the most of its content:

RECOMMENDATIONS FOR THE READER

To ensure you have a focused and meaningful reading experience, consider the following recommendations:

1. **Create a Comfortable Environment:** Make sure you are in a quiet, comfortable space that allows you to concentrate fully on the book. This will help you engage more deeply with the content.

2. **Begin with a Short Prayer:** Start your reading with a brief prayer to prepare your heart and mind to receive insights from the Word. This sets a reflective tone for your reading session.

3. **Have a Pen Ready:** Keep a pen handy to take important notes. Writing down key points or personal reflections will enhance your understanding and retention of the material.

4. **Revisit Difficult Sections:** If you encounter a paragraph or concept that you don't fully understand, don't rush past it. Re-read the section to ensure you grasp the message before moving on.

5. **Choose Your Underlining Tools Wisely:** If you want to underline passages in the book, consider using erasable markers or a #2 pencil. This allows you to make corrections without damaging the text.

6. **Utilize Post-Its:** Use post-it notes to jot down ideas or revelations. You can stick them on relevant pages for easy reference later, ensuring that important insights stay fresh in your mind.

7. **Meditate on What You Read:** Take time during the day to reflect on what you've read. Consider how the concepts apply to your life and relationships.

8. **Document Feedback:** If you receive any feedback or insights from others regarding the book's content, write it down in a notebook. This will help you track your thoughts and growth throughout your reading journey.

By following these recommendations, you will be better equipped to engage with the book meaningfully and implement its teachings into your life.

PERSONAL QUESTIONS FOR THE READER

1. What can I learn today?
2. What purposes does God have in my family?
3. What does God need me to change in my family?
4. What can I do to improve as a person?
5. What is my Purpose?
6. What do my children think of me?
7. What habits am I doing wrong in my family?
8. Am I satisfying my family as a parent?

QUESTIONS AND PURPOSE

1. What emotional state is your family in?
2. What spiritual state are your children in?
3. Have you taken the time to share the word and love of God with your children?
4. What marital status do your children have?(What are they distracted by?)
5. Have you taken the time to go out and talk with your children?
6. What Christ-centered habits do you have in your family?
7. Who influences your personal emotions?
8. How do you see your family today in 5 years?

PURPOSE

1. Grow in intimate relationship with God.
2. Mature spiritually and intellectually in God.
3. Grow and mature in relationship with your children.
4. Understand your children and support them in their difficult

times.
5. Change your thinking so that the glory of God is manifested in the family.
6. Write some personal resolutions for your children

.

Chapter 1

The Importance of Mutual Respect

Parents, do not exasperate your children, so that they do not become discouraged.

Colossians 3:21

16 Exasperate means:Hurt,irritate a painful or delicate part.
We often hear parents remind their children, "You must respect me because the Bible says, 'Honor your mother and father so that you may have long life.'" This phrase is commonly used to teach children the importance of respecting those who are raising them. While children may agree out of obedience, it often leads to a lingering tension beneath the surface.

Benito Juárez, a former president of Mexico, articulated that "between individuals, as between nations, respect for the rights of others is peace." This highlights that respect is not simply given; it is earned through consistent good behavior and conscious effort. Within the Christian community, a fundamental issue is often the repetition of scriptural verses without the practical application in daily life. We may read the Bible but fail to live by its teachings, neglecting God's Word.
Today marks a new chapter in understanding. Instead of merely citing verses, we should embody their principles in our lives. James 1:22-25 (NLT) reminds us, "Don't just listen to the word of God; you must put it into practice." This calls us to engage with our faith actively; simply hearing without acting serves to deceive ourselves.

Implementing God's Word manifests blessings that multiply. Children are not just additional members of the family; they are vital parts of our existence, born of us and deserving of our utmost care. Holy Scriptures refer to children as gifts from God, joyful rewards (Psalms 127:3-5 NLT). Realizing the blessing of parenthood is essential, as it is a treasure many long for but do not receive.

If you need motivation to improve your relationship with your children, understand their immense value. Just as one must carefully handle gold due to its fragility, so too must we nurture our children. God entrusts every parent with the responsibility to protect, guide, and teach children, establishing respect as a crucial pillar of this relationship. Respect demands attention towards those who possess wisdom, guiding us towards betterment.

Misconceptions about respect often arise where it's mistakenly viewed as something earned with age, leading to manipulation. This cultural misunderstanding has fueled discord between generations. Unfortunately, the consequences can manifest in troubling ways, including addiction and dangerous behaviors, as children bear the weight of their parents' failures.

To foster better connections, it's crucial to discard outdated cultural beliefs that hinder Jesus' teachings. Jesus emphasized the importance of self-denial in Mark 8:34-35 (NLT), reminding us that following him requires a shift in mindset that prioritizes love and compassion within the family unit.

Ultimately, Jesus distilled the essence of his teachings down to loving our neighbor as ourselves (Matthew 22:39 KJV), which extends beyond casual acquaintances to encompass our family members. Everyone's salvation is personal, underscoring that each person—partner and children alike—are neighbors deserving of love, as commanded by God.

In this light, fostering healthy communication and relationships rooted in respect and love can create an environment where families thrive.

FREQUENTLY ASKED QUESTION:

How can I respect my son,without losing respect for him?
Answer: God used the apostle Paul to write the fundamental formula of respect in 1Corinthians 13:4-8 saying this way:

Love is:
1. Patient.
2. Kind.
3. He is not jealous.
4. Braggart.
5. Proud.
6. Offensive.

7. He doesn't demand that things be done his way.
8. He does not get irritated or keep a record of the offenses received.
9. He does not rejoice in injustice but rejoices when the truth triumphs.
10. Love never gives up.
11. Never lose faith.
12. He always has hope.
13. It remains firm in all circumstances.

To truly grasp the concept of respect, one must first understand the significance of love. Love is the cornerstone that fosters respect; it establishes boundaries and cultivates self-control. In times of conflict, love helps prevent pride and arrogance from taking hold, promoting understanding and patience instead. The essence of respect can be found in love, admiration, and humility—without these qualities, respect cannot flourish.

Children deeply love parents who exhibit unconditional love and are ready to sacrifice for them. However, this love diminishes when parents display pride, arrogance, or a tendency to impose their will without compromise. A child's heart aches when faced with parents who refuse to listen, understand, or acknowledge their feelings. It feels like an unbearable weight, leading to frustration and exhaustion when communication breaks down due to stubbornness.

Children often feel powerless when they cannot express themselves without fear of disrespect. When parents yell or make hurtful comments, children are left feeling disappointed and neglected. Such negative interactions can lead to impulsive decisions driven by frustration. Regrettably, numerous children turn away from God, disillusioned by parents who disregard their feelings and dismiss their thoughts. Parents may argue that they're just trying to assert their authority, feeling offended by their children's words or actions. However, it's crucial to recognize that children struggle to process advice when they're hurting. They are not concerned with their parents' sacrifices or past experiences; they are navigating their own emotions.

Respect comes when parents demonstrate love over conflict, understanding over ignorance. Children appreciate it when, even during tough times, parents maintain an awareness of their emotional needs and allow them space to process their feelings. It's critical for parents to respect their children's boundaries, provided they do not endanger themselves or stray into harmful behaviors.

For a child, facing judgment from a parent can be excruciating and sometimes unforgivable. Parents need to recognize that harsh criticism, shouting, or insults are counterproductive. Instead, they should take on a counseling role, seeking to understand the root of their child's anxiety or struggles. Encouragement and constructive guidance help children learn and navigate challenges, rather than feeling judged and alone. When parents label their children's behavior without offering assistance, it creates deep emotional wounds. Children who feel judged internally, emotionally, and spiritually often spiral into depression, frustration, or isolation. They may even start to believe that their lives hold little worth, as the negative perceptions at home reinforce the harsh realities they face in the world. This leads many children to hide their struggles and seek compassion from others who may display understanding without judgment.

Children naturally possess kind hearts, but their emotional nourishment often suffers due to inadequate support from their parents. This needs to change, especially within the Christian community. It is disheartening to see parents lacking a strong foundation in faith, as Christian parents are called to be exemplary figures for those still seeking the truth. Unfortunately, there exists a divide within Christian circles, where some children choose to immerse themselves in the secular world, seeking solace and affirmation outside the home. The world may offer temporary comforts that parents sometimes neglect to provide. This situation should resonate deeply with every parent; it is a weighty spiritual concern. Above all other souls, parents must prioritize their children, for they are essential to the fabric of faith. It is possible that, on the day of judgment, the first souls held accountable may be those of their own children.

I ask you:
1.   What are you going to tell God about your children?
2.   Are you going to tell him that you cared more about the lost souls than those of your children?
3.   What excuse will you give to God?
4.   What did your children not want?
5.   What did they not want from God?

Children often turn away from God when their parents fail to reflect the loving and nurturing qualities of the Father. Many young people think, "If my parents act this way, I can't imagine what God must be like. I'd rather live my own life." This mindset often leads them to seek independence as soon as they reach adulthood, distancing themselves from their parents and, ultimately, from their faith.

This disconnection stems from a painful truth: while many parents may claim to follow the teachings of the Word, they sometimes only listen without truly putting those teachings into action. As a result, children bear the brunt of this inconsistency, leading to significant negative consequences.
It's crucial for parents to recognize the various factors that influence their children's behavior as they develop. While each child is unique, many can change for the worse due to several key reasons:

1. Lack of Parental Attention: Children thrive on attention and love from their parents. When they don't receive it, they may seek it elsewhere, sometimes in unhealthy ways.

2. Emotional or Verbal Hurt: Negative words or actions from parents can cause lasting damage. Children remember these moments and may struggle with self-worth as they grow.

3. Indifference: A lack of engagement or emotional connection can breed resentment and a sense of isolation in children. They may feel that their parents don't care about their lives and struggles.

4. Abuse of Authority: When parents treat their children as subordinates instead of individuals deserving respect, it leads to rebellion rather than harmony.

5. Neglecting Spiritual Education: Without moral guidance, children may lack the tools to navigate life's challenges, leading them to make poor choices.
These factors contribute to the turmoil many children experience, resulting in altered personalities and troublesome behaviors.

As a parent, you must understand that a child's perceived misbehavior is often a reflection of what they have absorbed from their environment, particularly from home. It's vital to take responsibility for the upbringing and acknowledge that the seeds you plant will bear fruit, good or bad.

Additionally, some parents may mistakenly believe they are doing well simply because their children don't outwardly display issues like homelessness or poverty. However, the reality is that while they might not be on the streets, they could be facing serious challenges at home, such as addiction to pornography, struggles with depression, or unhealthy relationships with technology or food. These hidden battles can stem from a lack of guidance or neglect in their upbringing.

Many parents fail to grasp the extent of their influence until they encounter the fallout from their children's struggles. Unfortunately, this often comes too late, after the damage is done.

In today's culture, some parents believe that providing electronic devices without supervision or limits is acceptable.

They might think, "As long as I can see them and they aren't doing anything outwardly wrong, they're fine." However, this mindset neglects the deeper issues at play. It's essential to strike a balance and set clear boundaries, fostering healthy habits that align with both physical and spiritual well-being. Ultimately, nurturing a strong, respectful relationship with children requires active involvement, love, and consistent guidance. By embodying the qualities of respect and care, parents can help their children grow into individuals who not only respect themselves but also have a genuine relationship with God.

WAKE UP!! This is the number one mistake that parents are making today! Believing that children cannot be influenced because they are at home is a lie! Influence today is no longer determined by what they do outside their home or physical treatment; rather, it is managed by social networks that are shaping our children through videos and experiences they can access without leaving the house.

It is impossible, and should not be tolerated, for parents to make friends with ignorance. If there is anything that needs to be done, it is to update their knowledge regarding electronics and emotions. It is no longer valid to say, "I don't know how to use the phone or the computer; those things are not for me." No! It is time for parents to take responsibility and begin to learn how to manage electronic devices so they can have greater control over their children's electronic activities.

The number one enemy of parents is ignorance. The more it is accepted, the more children suffer. The more ignorance there is, the more difficult it becomes to resolve issues. Parents need to be at the forefront of their knowledge of the new trends that young people engage with, to filter the influences affecting their children and provide parental support. Don't distance yourself from your children when you feel overwhelmed; instead, work on improving yourself and your understanding of the new generations.

Improving your quality as a person and updating your knowledge will empower you to reflect on and correct the mistakes you've made as a parent. It will also allow you to be humble enough to ask your children for forgiveness for any negative actions, behaviors, or words you may have directed toward them.

1. Do not throw your children out of the house because they did something wrong,they do it because there is something in them that you as a parent did wrong.It is impossible for a father who does things well to have children who do things wrong.
2. Don't chase your children away for not knowing how to work,it's your fault.
3. Don't chase your children away for being irresponsible,it's your fault.
4. Don't chase your children away for being poorly educated,it's your fault.
5. Don't kick your kids out for being lazy,it's your fault.
6. Don't kick your kids out for having bad grades,it's your fault.
7. Don't chase your children away for disrespecting you,it's your fault.
8. Don't blame your kids for using drugs,it's your fault.
9. Don't chase your children away for not seeking God,it's your fault.
10. Don't kick your kids out for playing video games all day,it's your fault.
11. Don't kick your kids out for using the computer all day,it's your fault.
12. Don't chase your children away for skipping school,it's your fault.
13. Don't chase your children away for drinking alcoholic beverages,i t's your fault.
14. Don't chase your children away for going to bars and nightclubs, it's your fault.

"Our children are too sensitive," or "They need to toughen up," or even "This is how we were raised, so this is how they should be." These phrases may seem harmless or even traditional, but they often inflict emotional wounds that can last a lifetime. Children are impressionable, and the words we use carry weight that can shape their self-esteem and outlook on life.

As parents, we have a responsibility to break these patterns and cultivate an environment where our children feel valued, respected, and loved. This means offering guidance that is firm but compassionate, understanding their needs, and actively engaging in their emotional development. Instead of dismissing their feelings, we should encourage open dialogue, allowing them to express themselves freely. It is essential to create a safe space where they know they are heard and understood.

Raising children requires intention—it involves being present in their lives and having the courage to lead them in a positive direction, even when it's challenging. This commitment to your children's well-being can create a ripple effect, positively impacting future generations. By setting high standards and teaching them the importance of hard work, integrity, and resilience, you empower them to navigate life's challenges successfully.

Moreover, aligning our parenting approach with principles rooted in love and understanding as reflected in the teachings of God, we can foster a deep-seated sense of purpose and belonging within our children. They will grow up recognizing their inherent value and understanding how to treat others with kindness and respect.

Investing in our children's emotional and spiritual health is not just a gift to them; it's a legacy we build for future generations. When we prioritize love and instruction over distraction and neglect, we set a solid foundation for them to thrive.

Let us rise above societal norms that perpetuate negativity. By being proactive and embracing a mindset of growth and positivity, we can profoundly influence our children's lives, ensuring they grow into individuals who contribute positively to the world. It's never too late to start this journey; let's challenge ourselves to make a difference in our families and, by extension, in our communities by not using phrases like

"You are useless!"
"You are just like your mother(or father)!"
"So,when are you going to be someone in life?!"
"You are a zero !"
"You are a stuge!"
"You are an idiot!"
"You never get anything done!"
"You are a disgrace!"
"You will never be anything in this life!"
"You don't stand a chance!"
"You are retarded!"
"You are incapable!"
"You never will!"

When we reflect on the power of our words, it becomes evident that they play a crucial role in shaping the lives of our children. The implications of what we say can be profound; it's not just about the immediate context, but also the long-term effects those words can have on their self-image, aspirations, and overall mindset. What may seem like simple jokes or lighthearted comments can unconsciously plant seeds of doubt or negativity that bloom into lasting challenges.

As followers of Christ, we are called to be mindful of our speech. Our words should be a source of encouragement and strength for our children, fostering an environment where they can thrive. We must strive to speak blessings, affirmations, and words of life into their hearts. This not only nurtures their development but also instills a sense of purpose and confidence that will guide them through life's hurdles.

James makes an important observation about the dual nature of our speech, revealing how inconsistent it can be. We often find ourselves in situations where we offer praise one moment and criticisms the next. This inconsistency can create confusion and emotional turmoil for our children. Instead, we should aim for a steady stream of positive reinforcement, drawing from the well of wisdom found in the Word of God.

To change our vocabulary, we need to engage in self-reflection and diligence. This process starts with prayer, asking God to give us the insight to identify those negative patterns. With His help, we can develop self-control and discipline in our speech, casting off words that bring harm and replacing them with those that uplift and inspire.

This commitment to change will not only benefit our children but will also serve as an example for them to follow. By modeling this behavior, we teach them the importance of verbal kindness and the weight of their own words. They will learn to avoid the pitfalls of negative speech and to embrace a life of affirmation and encouragement.

Let's be intentional in cultivating a home where love and positivity thrive. Investing in the power of our words can transform the atmosphere of our families and lay a solid foundation for our children's futures. It is never too late to begin this journey—each day offers a new opportunity to speak life into the hearts of those we cherish. By doing so, we are not only changing our families' narratives but also creating a legacy of love and strength that will endure for generations to come.

"Human beings can tame all kinds of animals,birds,reptiles and fish,but no one can tame the tongue.It is evil and tireless,full of deadly poison.Sometimes he praises our Lord and Father,and other times he curses those whom God created in his own image.And so,the blessing and the curse come out of the same mouth.Surely,my brothers,that is not right!Can sweet water and bitter water flow from the same spring?Can a fig tree bear olives or a vine fig?No,any more than one can draw fresh water from a salty spring"(James 3:7-12 NLT).

FREQUENTLY ASKED QUESTION:

What words can I use to motivate my child?

Answer:
These affirmations are powerful and can significantly impact a child's self-esteem and motivation. By consistently expressing such positive beliefs, we reinforce their potential and encourage a strong sense of self-worth.
When children hear phrases like:
- "You are a champion!"
- "You are better than your mother and I combined!"
- "You are going to become someone very important in life!"
- "You are an immense gift to our lives!"
- "You're extraordinary!"
- "Keep it up, and you will become someone in life!"
- "Everything you set your mind to, you will achieve!"
- "You are a spectacular person!"

they internalize these messages, which helps shape their identity and aspirations. These words not only uplift them but also create a positive atmosphere in the home, fostering resilience and ambition.

As parents, it's crucial to celebrate their achievements, both big and small, and to remind them of their unique qualities and capabilities. Such encouragement empowers them to pursue their passions and believe in their ability to overcome obstacles.

Ultimately, weaving these affirmations into everyday conversations and interactions can build a strong foundation for healthy emotional development. It nurtures their confidence and equips them to face life's challenges with optimism. Recognizing their worth and potential from an early age can inspire them to strive for greatness, ultimately leading them to become the remarkable individuals they are meant to be.

Don't abandon them:
In the hustle and bustle of life, it's easy for some parents to inadvertently neglect their children, especially when faced with

their mistakes. This can be a grave error. Abandoning a child in their moments of struggle reveals a lack of sensitivity and inconsistency in parenting.

Consider this: If God stands by you during your toughest times —when you feel overwhelmed by debt, hunger, scarcity, pain, or anguish—why would you choose to abandon your children in their times of need? What distinguishes your relationship with God from the relationship you have with your children? The answer is straightforward: there is no difference!

The bond you share with your children mirrors the unconditional love that God extends to us. Our Heavenly Father is a perfect example of unwavering support and love. Just as He does not abandon us, we must also remain steadfast for our children.

- If God does not leave you without food, then neither should you leave your children wanting.
- If God does not cast you out into homelessness, you must provide a secure home for your children.
- If God forgives your missteps, make sure to extend that same forgiveness to your child.
- If God continually cares for you, reflect that care in your actions towards your children.
- If God offers you shelter, ensure that your children always feel safe and secure in your home.
- If God embraces you when you feel unloved, take the time to express that love and compassion to your children.
- If God delivers you from evil, be there to guide your children through their own struggles.

In essence, let God's example be your guide. Nurturing your relationship with your children is crucial, just as your relationship with God is vital. By demonstrating unwavering love, support, and forgiveness, you teach your children the values they need to carry forward in their lives. In doing so, you create a strong, loving foundation for them, encouraging them to thrive despite challenges.

Jesus said:*"You who are parents,if your children ask you for a fish,do you give them a snake instead?Or if they ask for an egg, Do you get a scorpion?Of course not!"(Luke 11:11-12 NLT)*.

Don't give "scorpions and snakes" to your children; in other words, don't act out of selfishness. It's essential to remember that when conflicts arise between you and your partner, or in any difficult situation, your children are still observing and absorbing everything around them. The Word of God teaches us the importance of forgiveness and healing, urging us to mend relationships for the well-being of everyone involved.
The Scriptures remind us that:

- Forgiveness is essential: Just as God forgives us our transgressions, we must also forgive one another. This allows for healing and renewal within our family. Holding onto grievances only breeds resentment and negativity, which can harm our children emotionally and spiritually.

- Unity is crucial Strive to maintain a united front even during disagreements. Presenting a stable and harmonious environment gives your children the security they need to flourish. It helps them understand that relationships require effort, communication, and forgiveness.

- Words matter: When you argue or express conflict, be mindful of the language you use. Avoiding harsh words and negative comments will prevent them from feeling caught in the middle or developing a skewed perspective on relationships.
- Set an example: Children learn by observing us. When they see parents actively seek reconciliation and demonstrate love and understanding, they are more likely to replicate those behaviors in their lives.

In summary, prioritize forgiveness and create a nurturing environment where love prevails over conflict. By doing so, you will equip your children with the tools they need to handle their own relationships in a healthy manner. The teachings of the

Word guide us toward building a family bond that reflects grace, understanding, and unconditional love.

"When you are praying,first forgive everyone against whom you hold a grudge,so that your father in heaven may also forgive you your sins"(Mark 11:25 NLT).

God cannot forgive your sins if you do not forgive those of your children. To embrace true forgiveness, you must set aside selfishness, pride, and arrogance. Only by forgiving their offenses can you freely approach God and seek His forgiveness without barriers. As the saying goes, "First things first."Children are incredibly perceptive, and they will respect you
when you show respect for their feelings, emotions, and perspectives—even when you might be wrong. The respect they seek is not too much to ask; it is a reciprocal relationship. Avoid letting pride stand in the way of this crucial connection because losing their trust and respect is not worth it.

Remember: children are invaluable—they represent the future and are worth every sacrifice. As President Benito Juárez wisely noted, "Among individuals, as between nations, respect for the rights of others is peace." If you desire a peaceful relationship with your children, it begins with giving them the respect they rightfully deserve. This mutual respect forms the bedrock of a healthy relationship, fostering an environment where love and understanding cathrive.

Additionally, when your child makes a mistake, approach the situation with care. Instead of scolding or punishing them, take the time to explain where they went wrong. This instructional approach fosters respect and trust, showing them that you care about their growth rather than merely enforcing rules.
Mistreating or belittling your children can lead to feelings of hatred and resentment.

Remember: God entrusted you with these precious lives to nurture and instruct, not to destroy their spirit. You play a vital role in shaping their understanding of the world, their self-esteem, and their future relationships.

Prioritize love, instruction, and respect in your parenting. By doing so, you create a nurturing environment where your children can thrive and grow into respectful and responsible individuals. You are indeed a pivotal piece in their lives, and your influence holds tremendous power.

Chapter 2

You are a Super Hero

Parents, do not exasperate your children, so that they do not become discouraged.

Colossians 3:21

Exasperate means:Cause great irritation or anger.
Every person has a concept of what a hero is. Shows, movies, books, and even toys illustrate these ideas, often highlighting their appearance. However, true heroism lies not in how one looks but in the actions they take for others, often placing their own interests aside.

As a child, I was fortunate to have a father who worked hard to provide for us and a mother who devoted her days to caring for us. They instilled in me the values of hard work and sacrifice. My mother took us to visit my grandparents, and during those evenings spent watching western movies together, we formed lasting memories. My grandfather, who grew up at the beginning of the 20th century, loved to sit with us and enjoy those films, often offering us a glass of cold tea he brewed himself. To this day, that drink evokes fond memories of our time together.

I recall a moment when my uncle Larry introduced us to Zorro. Curious about the film, I asked him what it was about. He explained that Zorro was a superhero who wore a cape and stood up against the injustices of the government, saving those in need. As we watched the VHS, I was captivated by Zorro's courageous actions, battling foes while protecting the innocent. The way he faced danger head-on, often in formidable situations, left a profound impression on me.

Zorro personified a hero—not just for his skills but for his unwavering commitment to justice and the well-being of those around him. His bravery and eloquence in confronting the governor and standing up for what was right resonated deeply within me. It taught me that no matter how daunting the challenge, preparation and determination can lead to victory.
Heroes have this unique ability to leave a lasting impact on our lives. They shape our perspectives, teaching us kindness and compassion for those in need.

In this chapter, I aim to share the perspective of a child about parents. If you are reading this book, it's likely because you seek to bridge the gaps in your relationship with your child, whether due to distance, lack of love, or issues such as rebellion and substance abuse.

Today provides a golden opportunity for you to step into the role of your child's superhero. But before moving forward, I encourage you to engage in self-reflection. This journey of self-analysis can help unveil the root of the problems, setting the stage for healing and connection. By taking this step, you can become the hero your child needs, demonstrating that love and support can overcome even the most significant challenges.

Self-analysis:

How many times have you listened to your child when he asked you to speak?

How many times have you saved your child from an accident without scolding him?

How many times have you helped your child without asking for anything in return?

How many times have you taken time to go play sports with him and take the opportunity to talk for a while?

How many times have you made the effort to show him that he can trust you to talk about anything without defrauding the trustworthiness he has in you?

Children are drawn to superheroes because these characters embody a deep concern for the well-being of others. They soar through the skies, engage in epic battles, and face daunting challenges not for their own gain but to protect and uplift those around them. This profound dedication to others serves as a powerful example of selflessness.

In this spirit, I want to highlight some key areas where you might be falling short in your relationship with your children. Recognizing these points can be the first step toward meaningful change. By focusing on these aspects, you can transform not only your children's lives but also your relationship with them and their future.

1. Active Listening: Ensure you're truly hearing what your children have to say. Sometimes, amidst our busy lives, we forget to listen actively. Show them that their thoughts and feelings matter.
2. Quality Time: Make a concerted effort to spend quality time with your children. This could be as simple as playing a game, sharing a meal, or engaging in conversations. The time you invest in them builds trust and connection.

3. Emotional Support: Be there for your children emotionally. Validate their feelings and concerns, whether they're facing challenges at school or struggles with friendships. Show them that it's okay to feel and express emotions.

4. Lead by Example: Children learn by observing. Strive to be a role model in how you handle challenges, communicate effectively, and treat others. Your actions speak louder than words.

5. Encouragement and Affirmation: Uplift your children with words of encouragement. Celebrate their successes, no matter how small, and help them learn from setbacks. Your belief in them can fuel their self-confidence.

6. Set Boundaries with Love: Establishing rules and boundaries is essential, but ensure you do it with love and understanding. Explain the reasons behind your decisions and involve them in setting those rules.

7. Be Present: In a world filled with distractions, being present can be a powerful gift. Put away devices during family time and engage fully with your children.

By focusing on these key areas, you can create a healthier, more loving environment that mirrors the selflessness of a superhero. Every positive change you make in your relationship with your children can make a profound difference in their lives and futures. Remember, it's never too late to become the superhero they need, offering them love, support, and guidance as they navigate their own journeys.

Step 1: The Word of God emphasizes the importance of instructing our children from a young age, ensuring they have the necessary foundations to become responsible and loving parents themselves. As it says in Proverbs 22:6 (NLT), "Lead your children on the right path, and when they grow old, they will not abandon it."

The term "lead" carries significant meaning, which can be broken down into three key aspects:

1. To cause a moving thing to move in a certain direction without diverting: This means that as parents, we have the responsibility to guide our children steadfastly toward positive values and principles. Just as a ship is steered toward its destination, we must ensure that our children stay focused on their path and not be swayed by distractions.

2. To place an established address: This indicates the importance of creating a stable and secure environment at home. By helping our children understand where they come from and what values we stand for, we establish a foundation that they can refer back to throughout their lives.

3. Direct it toward a specific point: This encourages us to set clear goals and expectations for our children. By directing them toward specific values, beliefs, and behaviors, we prepare them to navigate the complexities of life with purpose and confidence.

Instructing your children in this manner requires intentionality and consistency. By actively engaging in their upbringing and modeling the behaviors you wish to see, you help them forge their paths. Ultimately, this guidance is essential in cultivating a generation that embodies love, kindness, and responsibility. It's a powerful commitment that shapes not only their present but also their future as parents and community members

"Train up a child in the way he should go,and even when he is old,he will not depart from it"(KJV).

The word instruct means:
1. To teach
2. To Provide knowledge and systematically communicate knowledge or doctrines.
One of the many reasons why children need "superhero" parents is due to their lack of personal direction. Children, tweens, and young people navigate a complex journey that often tests their self-confidence and faith in their abilities.

During these formative years, they are faced with decisions that can lead to mistakes—choices that may have been avoided with proper guidance. Unfortunately, when there is a lack of direction, these decisions often turn out to be the wrong ones.

This situation often stems from parental irresponsibility. It's important to recognize that the influence of a pastor, teachers, or friends is not the primary cause of our children's poor decisions. The Word of God provides us with clear guidance on this matter: "Parents, do not make your children angry by the way you treat them. Rather, raise them with the discipline and instruction that comes from the Lord" (Ephesians 6:4 NLT).

This scripture emphasizes the critical role that parents play in their children's lives. It highlights the need for parents to take on the responsibility of nurturing and guiding their children. It encourages us to be attentive and proactive, correcting and instructing them in each step they take. This attention to detail is essential for building a solid foundation that helps them navigate life's challenges more effectively.

Being a superhero parent means being involved, providing direction, and teaching them how to make sound decisions. When children know they have parents who genuinely care and are dedicated to their growth, they feel more secure and are better equipped to face obstacles. By instilling discipline and values rooted in love and understanding, you empower them to build their self-confidence and discernment, ultimately guiding them toward making wise choices throughout their lives.

FREQUENT QUESTIONS:
What do I do if my children are already grown?

God's response to parents is: "Parents,do not make your children angry with the way you treat them.Rather,raise them with the discipline and instruction that comes from the Lord"(Ephesians 6:4 NLT).
What does God say to my children?

God's response to children is: "Children,obey your parents because you belong to the Lord,for this is right."Honor your father and your mother."That is the first commandment that contains a promise:if you honor your father and mother,"it will be well with you,and you will have a long life in the land""(Ephesians 6:1-3 NLT).
What do I gain by correcting my children?

God's response to parents is:
"Discipline your children,and they will give you peace of mind and gladden your heart"(Proverbs 29:17 NLT).

Being a superhero in your child's life involves a combination of guidance, support, and unconditional love. Here are some ways you can embody that role:

1. Lead by Example: Children often imitate their parents' behavior. By demonstrating positive values and healthy habits, you can inspire your child to adopt the same.

2. Communicate Openly: Foster a safe space for open dialogue. Listen actively to your child's thoughts and feelings, and provide them with age-appropriate explanations about the world

.

3. Set Goals Together: Help your child identify their interests and aspirations. Set achievable goals and work with them to create a plan to reach those goals. Celebrate their progress, no matter how small.

4. Teach Resilience: Life will bring challenges, and it's important for children to learn how to cope with setbacks. Encourage them to view failures as opportunities for growth and learning.

5. Instill Values: Share the values and beliefs significant to your family. Teach your child about respect, kindness, perseverance, and empathy, guiding them to understand the importance of these qualities.
6. Provide Support and Guidance: Be there to support your child's decisions while also guiding them toward what is right. Offer advice when needed but allow them to make choices and learn from the consequences.

8. Encourage Independence: Allow your child to take age-appropriate risks and make their own decisions. This fosters confidence and teaches them responsibility.

9. Spend Quality Time: Engage in activities together that you both enjoy. This not only strengthens your bond but also creates lasting memories.
10. Model Healthy Relationships: Demonstrate how to maintain positive relationships through effective communication and conflict resolution.

11. Connect with God: Incorporate spiritual practices into your family life, such as prayer or reading religious texts together. This can provide guidance and reinforce values.

By actively participating in your child's life and showing them love and mentorship, you become their superhero, guiding them toward a fulfilling and purposeful life.

Adding to what has been said,God gives us

step#2 which is:
"You must commit with your entire being to fulfill each of these mandates that I give you today.Repeat to your children repeatedly.Talk about them in your conversations when you are at home and when you are on the road,when you go to bed and when you get up.Tie them to your hands and wear them on your forehead as a reminder.Write them on the doorposts of your house and on the gates of the city"(Deuteronomy 6:6-9 NLT).

You can be a superhero to your children without the need to use force. Use the Stratagies!

ALWAYS REMEMBER:

¡A superhero doesn't scold,he guides!
¡A superhero doesn't hit,he corrects!
¡A superhero always helps without expecting anything in return!
¡The children hurt No need violence,need love!

Reminder:

1Corinthians 13:4-7(NLT)
1.   Love is patient and kind.
2.   Love is not jealous,nor boastful,nor proud,nor offensive.
3.   He doesn't demand that things be done his way.
4.   He does not get irritated or keep a record of the offenses received.
5.   He does not rejoice in injustice but rejoices when the truth triumphs.
6.   Love never gives up.
7.   Never lose faith.
8.   He always has hope.
9.   It remains firm in all circumstances.

YOUR CHILDREN NEED YOU TO:

Embody patience and understanding as they navigate their mistakes. It's essential to approach them with caution, especially in moments of frustration, to model calm and respectful communication. Being open to their advice can also strengthen your relationship, showing them that their thoughts and feelings matter.

Humility is key—listen without judgment and refrain from resorting to lies while guiding them. Always take the time to hear their side of things before forming conclusions. It's vital to maintain unwavering belief in their potential, as they rely on your support and encouragement, especially during difficult times.

In these current dangerous times, parental involvement is crucial. If you don't step in, who will? Friends may offer misguided influences, and harmful habits can arise from boredom and isolation. It's critical to stay engaged with your children to counteract the challenges presented by depression and anxiety, which are rampant among youth today.

This is your moment to actively listen to their issues, to deeply engage with them, and to start pulling out the roots of Resentment, pain, and frustration that may be hiding beneath the surface. With love, understanding, and dedication, you can participate in their healing. Your affection—through hugs, kind words, and encouragement—will provide them with the comfort they desperately need.

They don't need harsh reminders of their mistakes; they long for heartfelt words of hope and affirmation. They want to hear that everything will be okay, that you believe in them, and that you will always be there to support their dreams.

If expressing love or compassion feels difficult, turn to God for strength and wisdom. Ask for help in softening your heart to better serve your children's needs. You hold the key to helping them overcome their struggles, whether it's with addiction, depression, or anxiety.

It's never too late to make a significant difference in their lives and, by extension, in your family. Take this opportunity to be the superhero they need—today can be the start of healing and positive change for your family!

———

Chapter 3

Take Care of Moral Discipline

Discipline your children, and they
will give you peace of mind
and they will gladden your heart.

Proverbs 29:17

Julio Cesar Chavez Sr. once said, "I know it is very difficult, but with discipline, perseverance, dedication, and a lot of effort, you are able to achieve your goals." This wisdom is especially relevant for parents aiming to transform their child's life. To make a significant impact, it's crucial to establish four foundational principles: discipline, perseverance, dedication, and a commitment to consistent effort.

Good parents aren't born; they are made through intentional actions and choices. To fully understand your child's perspective, you must cultivate discipline in your day-to-day life. Children dealing with personal issues often feel defensive and sensitive, responding to their environment with unease.

Today's realities are different from those two decades ago. The prevalence of technology and the openness of society in sharing knowledge have dramatically shaped younger generations. Social networks play a pivotal role in their everyday lives, and parents must recognize their influence as both a potential asset and a double-edged sword. Without proper guidance and internal discipline within the home, children can be easily swayed by negative external influences.
A strong home, filled with positive parental guidance rooted in discipline, perseverance, effort, and dedication, fosters a healthy and resilient relationship between parents and children. To truly empathize with your child, you need to "put yourself in their shoes." Utilizing common sense is crucial to this understanding.

The senses—sight, sound, smell, touch, and taste—affect how the brain processes experiences. Unfortunately, negative influences often target these senses to ensnare young people in harmful behaviors. The adversary understands that if a child's common senses are stimulated in line with their vulnerabilities, it can significantly damage their mind, heart, and spirit.

Awareness of this process allows parents to be proactive in safeguarding their children. By instilling strong values and providing a nurturing environment, you can help them navigate the complexities of today's world, ensuring that they are equipped to resist negative influences. Reinforcing the importance of healthy communication and understanding will empower them to make positive choices. Your role as a parent is paramount in fostering resilience and strength within them as they face external challenges.

LISTEN "The serpent was the most cunning of all the wild animals that the Lord God had made.One day he asked the woman:"Did God really tell you that you should not eat the fruit of any of the trees in the garden?"(Genesis 3:1 NLT).

The reality is that negative influences can deeply impact our children, especially when they are surrounded by people who do not share the same values. The enemy seeks to plant seeds of curiosity, using various tactics to draw them away from their faith and integrity. It's vital for parents to remain vigilant against these attempts to undermine their children's innocence and peace of mind.

A report from Top News highlighted in 2015 revealed concerning statistics about adolescents aged 15 to 18: most high school students received education on pregnancy prevention, sexually transmitted diseases, and contraception. While it's essential for young people to be informed, this focus on sexual education underscores a shift that parents should be aware of. Schools increasingly address topics that historically fell under parental guidance, and this can create a disconnect between the values taught at home and those presented in an educational setting.

If parents are not proactive in these discussions, schools may inadvertently convey that living with integrity, according to God's teachings, is outdated or narrow-minded. There's a risk that children may be led to believe that God is irrelevant or that biblical principles are mere fiction.

It is the responsibility of parents to instill a sense of faith and values in their children, guiding them in the fear of the Lord as they navigate today's challenges. Without this guidance, the world will fill that void with messages that lead away from God. As a parent, you have a choice: you can engage in these crucial conversations and teach your children about their faith, or you can risk allowing external influences to define their beliefs and actions.

The foundation you build now will significantly impact the issues your children face as adolescents and teenagers. Prioritizing open discussions about integrity, morality, and spirituality will empower your children to make informed choices and seek a path aligned with their faith. It is crucial to be present and involved in their education, ensuring they understand the importance of their beliefs in a world filled with conflicting messages. You have the power to shape their worldview and protect their innocence by standing firm in your role as a guiding influence in their lives.

SEE "And the woman saw that the tree was good for food,and that it was pleasant to the eyes,and a desirable tree to make one wise;"(Genesis 3:6 NLT

The reality is that the enemy is adept at using appealing distractions to ensnare our children. Temptations such as pornography, illicit activities, and the lure of easy money are common traps designed to draw them away from their integrity and relationship with God. We see this reflected in social media, where individuals flaunt wealth gained through questionable means, normalizing a lifestyle that can lead to moral decay.

In a world increasingly desensitized to such vices, it becomes essential to educate our children about these temptations. For those who lack a foundation in God's teachings, the allure of exposing their personal lives or succumbing to societal pressures can be overwhelming. It's heartbreaking to witness how many young people, including those from Christian backgrounds, fall into the depths of drug addiction and sin. Some are lost to their struggles, facing imprisonment or even death. This is particularly disheartening for families devoted to serving God; we must be proactive in safeguarding our children from such outcomes.

We cannot allow the negativity and debauchery of the world to infiltrate our Christian families. There must be a clear distinction between those who follow God and those who embrace worldly pleasures. Raising the "flag of war" involves advocating for our children, helping them understand why Christians live differently than those who seek fulfillment through materialistic or harmful choices. We must fight for the souls of our children, instructing and leading them in the fear of God.

It's crucial to engage actively in their upbringing, ensuring they grasp the importance of their faith and the reasons behind living a life aligned with God's values. The challenges the world presents can seem like offerings on a silver platter, but with dedicated parental guidance and education, children can learn to reject these enticements. By instilling strong principles and encouraging them to embrace their faith, parents have the power to guide their children on a path that honors their integrity and draws them closer to God. This mission is vital—not only for our own children but for all young people, as we strive to create a brighter and more faithful future.

TOUCH

"And he took of its fruit and ate;and he gave also to her husband,who ate as well as her"(Genesis 3:6 NLT).

The enemy is indeed cunning and takes advantage of moments when children are away from their parents. In those vulnerable times, they are more susceptible to making poor decisions that can have long-lasting effects on their lives. It's during these opportune moments, when parental protection is lacking, that harmful influences and substances may seem most appealing. Therefore, parents must actively communicate the differences between right and wrong, ensuring their children understand the consequences of their actions.

It's also essential for parents to remain vigilant regarding the friendships their children choose. Teaching kids how to select friends wisely is a critical part of their development. Children need to learn that not everyone who calls themselves a friend has their best interests at heart. Associating with individuals who engage in negative behaviors can lead to stumbling blocks that impede their path to success. A true friend will uplift and encourage positive choices, while those who cause harm cannot truly be considered friends; they are merely acquaintances.

Parents should emphasize that anything detrimental to their physical, emotional, or spiritual well-being is essentially "forbidden fruit." Just as God instructed Adam and Eve regarding the trees in the Garden of Eden, today's children face various temptations in their own "garden of life." Understanding what to avoid will equip them to navigate their environment more safely.

It's vital to foster an atmosphere where knowledge and awareness are prioritized. Ignorance can lead to dangerous consequences, so remaining engaged in your children's lives is crucial. Regularly check in on their experiences, their friendships, and even their online interactions. Encouraging open conversations can help them feel safe to share their struggles and successes with you.

As a parent, your guidance can lead to a fulfilling and peaceful life for your children, helping them abide by God's promises and principles. Be proactive, be present, and most importantly, impart wisdom that will guide them through the challenges they will inevitably face. Your role is critical in helping them avoid pitfalls and embrace a path that honors their integrity and faith.

"Be alert!Beware of his great enemy,the devil,for he prowls around like a roaring lion,seeking someone to devour"

1 Peter 5:8(NLT)

Chapter 4

These are other times

No, beloved brothers, I have not achieved it, but I concentrate solely on this: I forget the past and fix my gaze on what lies ahead, and thus I advance until I reach the end of the race to receive the heavenly prize to which God calls us through Christ Jesus.

Philippians 3:13-14

The rapid pace of scientific advancement and technological innovation is transforming our lives in unprecedented ways. New ideas and inventions are emerging daily, and this technological revolution demands that society adapts and evolves quickly to keep pace. The COVID-19 pandemic of 2020 serves as a prime example of this necessity for adaptation. In just a few weeks, the world underwent dramatic changes, from the implementation of health protocols to shifts in how businesses operate, such as the surge in delivery services like Uber Eats and DoorDash.

These transformative moments highlight the importance of continuous growth within families. Just as our children eagerly anticipate the latest gadgets or gaming consoles, parents must also remain informed and receptive to new knowledge and trends. We must recognize that the context in which children are growing up today is vastly different from that of previous generations. Those who cling to outdated views risk leaving their families vulnerable to the challenges and dangers that arise in our rapidly changing world.

It is crucial for parents to keep in mind that neglecting to update one's understanding of societal changes can lead to severe consequences. We must act quickly to educate ourselves on the issues our children may face, from social pressures to the influence of technology on their lives. Simply assuming that children will be fine in today's world is a dangerous approach.

As we navigate this landscape, it is alarming to witness the rise of moral depravity and the normalization of harmful ideologies. The parallels to the times of Sodom and Gomorrah are distressing, with movements advocating for what many consider to be destructive values gaining traction. The erosion of respect and sound moral principles is evident, and it poses a significant threat not only to our families but to society as a whole.

In this environment, open dialogue and proactive parenting are more important than ever. We must engage with our children about the values we hold and the dangers present in society. By strengthening our relationships with them and teaching them discernment, we equip them to face challenges with wisdom and integrity.

Let us commit to being vigilant, knowledgeable, and proactive in our parenting. As society continues to evolve at a breakneck speed, we must not shy away from the difficult conversations that will prepare our children for a future that is fraught with challenges. Only through informed and engaged parenting can we hope to safeguard their well-being and help them navigate the complexities of today's world.

Dear Parent, It's essential now more than ever to stay informed and aware of the changing landscape around us. Each passing moment brings new challenges, and the world can seem increasingly dangerous. It's our responsibility as parents to protect and guide our children along the path of righteousness and justice. Do not allow the currents of this new society to penetrate the hearts and minds of your loved ones.

Use this crucial time to prepare and equip your children, grandchildren, relatives, and friends. We are facing unprecedented challenges, and the battle against the forces of evil, which have always existed, is now more visible than in any previous generation.

The lessons from the Bible remind us that the world can easily fall into chaos, as seen during the days of Noah. This is not the time to embrace ignorance; instead, we must stand as vigilant guardians, prepared to confront the spiritual battles that surround us. We are entering a period of great trial, where knowledge and understanding are vital.

Encourage yourself and those around you to delve deeper into the realities of our current day. Awareness of the subtle tactics and influences at play can arm you with the knowledge needed to educate and protect your children from harm. Your understanding and insight play a crucial role in their lives, and it's important not to retreat or avoid these conversations.

Now is when parents need to reclaim their roles as leaders within their homes. God has a plan for your family, one filled with hope and purpose that extends to future generations. Just as Jacob fought for a blessing, we too must strive for the well-being and spiritual health of our children.

We cannot cling to the past and believe that the challenges have faded away. The times have indeed changed, and we must adapt and move forward, seeking the ultimate reward that awaits us. The crown of life is not just a promise but a goal worth pursuing. As we navigate these difficult times, let's remain steadfast in our commitment to our families, recognizing the importance of nurturing their growth in faith and wisdom. Together, we can guide them through today's complexities and toward a brighter, more hopeful future.

Dear Parent, The days of your childhood, those moments when innocence was cherished, are rapidly fading away as technology continues to advance. It is essential that you remain vigilant regarding the well-being and safety of your children. Don't be misled by the assumption that just because they are at home, they are safe from harm. In today's digital age, children have access to communication tools—video calls, chat rooms, and smartphones—that can pose significant risks. With just a few taps on a screen, inappropriate situations can arise without them ever leaving the house.

Let's not overlook the reality we are currently facing. Prioritize the emotional and spiritual health of your family by being aware of the influences surrounding them. Remember that your children's peace and well-being depend on your guidance. Keep the metaphorical oil in your lamp replenished, ensuring that your family remains protected under God's grace. Seek continual spiritual nourishment for both yourself and your children.

Your presence is irreplaceable. Don't abandon them to their tasks or school projects. Engage with them actively and dedicate the quality time they need from you. It's crucial to understand that no device can replace the personal connection and guidance that a parent provides.

If the world is innovating its technology, you must innovate your approach to parenting as well. As Philippians 4:13 reminds us, we can do all things through Christ who strengthens us—do not let your guard down! The world is moving forward, and so can you.

If the education your children receive in school doesn't meet their needs, you must step in to provide the instruction and direction they require. Do not wait for external sources—jails, gangs, other parents, or teachers—to teach your children how to navigate life. God entrusted you with them because He believed in your ability to guide and nurture them. Open your ears to their challenges, give them love, support, and reassurance. Your affection is the antidote to the emptiness that the world may offer.

Chapter 5

The importance of transparancy

And now, beloved brothers, one more thing to finish. Focus on all that is true, all that is honorable, all that is just, all that is pure, all that is beautiful, and all that is admirable. Think of excellent and praiseworthy things.

Philippians 4:8

The character and maturity of individuals manifest in sincerity, loyalty, and education. Maintaining transparency in your relationship with your children fosters trust and personal growth for both you and them. As you navigate these times, remember that your role is vital in shaping their values and perspectives. Actively participate in their lives, and guide them lovingly toward a path of righteousness. Your influence can help them stand strong against the pressures of today's society.

Parents always wonder:
10. Why did my son become rebellious?
11. What did I do to my son to make him start behaving in such a way?
12. What do I have to do so that my son accepts me and listens to my advice without getting angry about what I say?
13. How can I be my son's friend and father at the same time?

Parents wrestling with these thoughts often find themselves in a cycle of frustration and despair, feeling trapped amid an overwhelming accumulation of issues at school, with teachers, on the streets, and even contemplating the loss of their children. It's a heartbreaking reality, not a fictional narrative. Many Christian parents face daily battles with their children and feel helpless in addressing these challenges. This struggle can lead to blocking common sense, making situations worse, often rooted in a lack of transparency.

When parents find themselves exhausted and overwhelmed, it's easy to feel as though the fault lies elsewhere—perhaps with their spouse, their pastor, or their children's friends. However, the hard truth is that the solution often begins at home, with the parents themselves. The reality is that your children reflect your words and actions. If their behavior is troubling, it's a signal that something may be amiss in how you're guiding them.

Children are inherently good and crave love, affection, understanding, and encouragement from their parents. When parents provide satisfaction in these emotional and spiritual areas, children are more likely to express gratitude and strive to please their parents in return. They want to make their parents happy and feel valued. Conversely, children can develop negative feelings towards their parents' actions—such as injustice, indifference, or harmful behavior.

Consider this: when a parent dismisses a child's feelings or shows indifference to their struggles, the child may misinterpret this as a lack of love or support. This can lead to rebellion or withdrawal, where the child feels they must fend for themselves emotionally. A simple example can illustrate this point.

Imagine a scenario where a parent rushes out the door daily, barely acknowledging their child's day or asking about their feelings. Over time, the child might feel neglected, leading to behavior issues, seeking attention elsewhere, or mimicking the hurried and dismissive attitude of their parent. On the other hand, a parent who takes time to engage daily—asking questions, offering words of encouragement, and showing genuine interest—fosters a bond that encourages positive behavior.

It's imperative for parents to reflect on their actions and approach to parenting. True progress often starts with honesty, sincerity, and the willingness to make changes for the better. Rather than looking outside for solutions, consider that the key to nurturing your child's well-being lies within the dynamics of your home. Recognizing this can be painful but ultimately liberating, paving the way for healing and a stronger parent-child relationship.

When I was about eight years old, I was in the second grade and filled with the kind of joy and ambition that only a child can possess. I was inspired by the accomplishments of my classmates and dreamed of receiving awards from both my school and my parents. I made it my goal to excel in everything I did, striving to fill my heart with satisfaction and fulfillment.

My second-grade teacher, Mrs. Putzik, played a significant role in instilling that inspiration within me. She was an older woman with a strong character, honesty, and a sincerity that was palpable. Her lessons extended beyond textbooks; they encompassed life lessons that motivated us to dedicate ourselves to our studies. She always recognized our efforts, celebrating our achievements with genuine applause, which encouraged us to work even harder.

I vividly remember her words during history class: "You must learn to be dedicated and disciplined in your studies so that you can be an outstanding student. You cannot go through life creating deceptions along the way. Work hard, and your prize will come to you. Focus on the prize." Those words ignited a fire within me, motivating me to do my absolute best. We competed in our classroom, eager to showcase our best grades and earn diplomas of recognition.

When report card day finally arrived, the excitement was palpable. We all opened our envelopes, hoping to see the fruits of our labor reflected in our grades. I was anxious to see my results, desperate to make my parents proud and receive their praise. I opened my envelope to find that I had earned very good grades, distinguishing myself as an outstanding student. I felt a rush of joy, imagining the proud smiles and hugs I would receive.

That evening, when my mom saw my grades, her happiness radiated through her smile. She enveloped me in a warm embrace, and I felt loved. Then, my dad came home. I remember that night clearly; he was tired from work but seemed happy as we shared dinner together. It was finally time to show him my grades.

I approached him eagerly after he finished eating, clutching my report card in my hand. "Dad, look what I brought! I got a lot of fours—it's the highest grade! I passed my class!" The moment felt electric, filled with anticipation. Yet, when he glanced at my grades, I was met with an unexpected reality. "I don't care about your grades. Don't bring me those papers; they're no use to me. What matters is that you're obedient."

In an instant, my heart sank. Those words pierced me like a dagger, leaving me feeling small and dejected. I walked away, tears welling in my eyes, feeling a mix of anger, confusion, and heartbreak. I went to my room, overwhelmed by the weight of disappointment. How could the person I looked up to the most hurt me so deeply?

That night was unbearable. I cried myself to sleep, turning away from the world and feeling an immense sense of betrayal from my father—my hero. My mother noticed my pain and came to comfort me. She hugged me tightly, But even her solace couldn't mend the wound that had been inflicted.

Days turned to weeks, and I carried the burden of my father's dismissive words with me everywhere. They echoed in my mind, haunting me during meals, playtime, and even in solitude. I struggled to understand why a small gesture of encouragement—a hug or a few positive words—felt so out of reach.

As the years passed, I eventually learned the importance of forgiveness. It took me a long time, filled with reflection and emotional growth, to heal from that painful experience. I had to discover motivation within myself, focusing on my own happiness and dedicating my efforts to personal satisfaction rather than seeking approval from my father.

Though I was no longer the same child who yearned for validation, I found strength in my resilience. The journey toward forgiveness was difficult, but I emerged with a better understanding of the complexities of relationships and the importance of nurturing positive communication. Ultimately, that experience taught me valuable lessons about the power of words, the necessity for kindness, and the importance of unconditional support in a parent-child relationship.

Do not repeat the mistakes of the past, especially those that can deeply wound your children. Be mindful of the words you choose, the gestures you make, and the decisions you take in the heat of the moment. Remember, your children are precious gifts from God, and you are blessed to have them in your life. It's crucial not to hurt their feelings or damage the positive image they have of you. A careless word, an aggressive gesture, or a moment of frustration can lead them down dark paths—substance abuse, rebellion, or a sense of worthlessness.

As their parent, you have the power to build or break their self-esteem. Your response to their behavior should be rooted in love, not anger. Even when they misbehave or test your patience, reflect on the fact that they are your children.

Approach them with understanding rather than harshness. Be firm in moral and corrective discipline, but soft in your emotional reactions. You may never fully grasp the extent of the pain that a single harsh word can inflict on a child's heart.
I urge you to take a moment for self-reflection. Evaluate your actions and consider how you've interacted with your family.

Think about the occasions when you may have shouted, reacted aggressively, or made hurtful comments. Being honest with yourself is crucial, as it serves as the foundation for healing. Write down the negative moments you have experienced with your children and how you behaved during those times.

Once you have listed these instances, take the time to analyze each one closely. Reflect on the feelings you might have unintentionally inflicted and the consequences of those moments. Consider the following as you continue this important self-assessment:

1. **What were the triggering circumstances?** Identify the situations that led to your negative responses. Understanding the context can help you avoid similar triggers in the future.

2. **How did your words/actions affect your child?** Think about the potential emotional impact your responses may have had on your children's mental well-being. Were your words dismissive, harsh, or damaging?

3. **What were your intentions?** Did you mean to discipline, or were you simply reacting out of frustration? Distinguishing intention from impact is vital.

4. **How can you make amends?** Consider steps you can take to repair the relationship. Apologizing, having open conversations, or even spending quality time together can facilitate healing.

5. **What positive strategies can you implement?** Identify proactive measures to improve communication and strengthen your bond. Perhaps set aside dedicated time for family discussions or engage in activities that foster connection and understanding.

As you reflect on these questions, remember that healing is a gradual process. Your willingness to recognize past mistakes and to commit to changing your behavior is key to fostering a nurturing environment for your children. By prioritizing emotional intelligence and demonstrating unconditional love, you can build a strong and supportive relationship that allows them to thrive.

Your role as a parent is not just to guide them, but to be a source of encouragement and strength, even in challenging times.

Reflect on the following:

QUESTIONS ABOUT YOUR CHILDREN'S ATTITUDE
1. How did you behave after that problem?
2. What changed in your child after the problem?

3. What habits have you developed after that bad moment?Has he disrespected you?
4. Has your child ignored your advice?
5. Has he been emotionally indifferent to you?
6. Have you raised your voice in recent discussions?
7. Has he disobeyed an order or a favor you have asked of him?

PERSONAL QUESTIONS:
8. What did you do after that problem?
9. Did you ask for forgiveness for your bad actions?
10. Did you try to talk to him to solve the problem?
11. Did you reach an agreement with him so that it does not happen again?
12. Did you ask God for forgiveness for having been indifferent to your son?
13. Did you regret your bad actions towards your children?
14. Did you change your way of communicating things?
15. Did you change as a person,or did you stay the same?

In the next few lines,answer the questions you just read,be honest and answer to yourself, what you have done?

Most parents tend to react and then forget, but children do not have that luxury. They are like living recorders, capturing every action, every word, every gesture, and every decision made regarding their behavior. These moments stick with them, ingrained in their memories, especially if apologies and reconciliations are never made.

It's essential to be transparent with yourself and acknowledge your shortcomings as a parent. Accept responsibility for the wounds you may have caused and make a conscious effort to begin mending those wounds. This process can be difficult, but it's necessary for fostering a healthier relationship with your children.

You might find yourself thinking, "I didn't do anything to deserve this reaction from my child; their behavior has nothing to do with me." However, it is crucial to realize that if your child is reacting in ways that concern you, it often stems from something that needs to be addressed. The most painful reality occurs when a parent fails to recognize their role in the situation, avoiding transparency, and neglecting to seek forgiveness for their mistakes.

While it is true that the Bible provides directives for parenting, which include disciplining and correcting our children, it's important to remember that these teachings should be approached with love and understanding. The Word of God can be challenging, but the Holy Spirit is always there to guide us toward truth and justice. By connecting with God and seeking His guidance, you can find the clarity and strength needed to resolve conflicts and heal your family's emotional wounds.

If you start this journey of reflection and reconciliation, I am confident that you will see a positive change in your children's behavior and outlook. Your efforts to create a nurturing environment will lead you to fulfill your desire to see them happy and successful in all aspects of their lives.

As you navigate your journey, I encourage you to keep in mind the powerful words of Scripture: "Confess your sins to one another and pray for one another, that you may be healed. The fervent prayer of a righteous person has much power and gives wonderful results." (James 5:16, NLT). This verse serves as a reminder of the importance of honesty, humility, and the healing power of prayer. Embrace it as you work toward building a stronger, healthier family dynamic.

"Confess your sins to one another and pray for one another,that you may be healed.The fervent prayer of a righteous person has much power and gives wonderful results."James 5:16(NLT)

FREQUENTLY ASKED QUESTIONS ON THE TOPIC:
How do I resolve offenses with my children?

Step#1:Recognize your failures,and write each one down in a notebook

Step#2: Repent for having committed the offenses

Step#3: Ask God for forgiveness for not treating your children like the treasure they are.

Step#4: Pray to God to give you the right words to reconcile with them.

Step#5: Schedule a date with your child,invite him to eat at a restaurant or even at your own home(If possible).Prepare a gift of peace,something that will make him feel good when you receive it.It will improve the result of your intention.You do not believe me?Read:Genesis 32 and 33.

Step#6: When you arrive at the place,do not rush,try to soften the atmosphere by asking"how is it?""How do you feel?""What have you done?"He tries to warm up the atmosphere by showing that you care about his well-being and health.

Step#7: Be clear,be direct.Don't turn the conversation around,it could be that your child will get bored and better leave or maybe you won't get to the main topic of everything.EYE!You may have nerves,but ignore them,your relationship with him is worth losing your pride.Above all,remember:

BETRANSPARENT,HONEST AND SINCERE!

Step#8: Ask Him for forgiveness for your offenses,be specific about which offenses.RECOMMENDATION:Carry that notebook with you so you can read the offenses for which you want to apologize and apologize.

Step#9: After you have asked each other for forgiveness,put James 5:1 into practice.Pray together.Make a prayer for peace,touch God's heart to strengthen your family relationship.

Step#10: Give your child a sincere hug and kiss, and express to them just how much you love and want them in your life. Take the time to tell them how much you truly care. Share words of hope, encouragement, and love. If that hug feels like it needs to last a little longer, don't hesitate—stay there, wrapped in that moment with your child.

These moments are incredibly powerful; they hold the potential to heal emotional wounds. They create lasting memories and foster a sense of security and belonging. When you embrace your child with genuine affection, you are communicating that they matter, that they are valued, and that they can always turn to you for support.

Such simple yet profound gestures can radically change a child's perspective. They help children recognize their purpose, instill confidence, and uplift them, no matter where they currently stand in their lives. Through love and connection, you can guide them toward resilience and self-worth, reminding them that they are never alone in their journey.
Transparency comes with a price, and it's a price worth considering. You might be asking yourself, "What is that price?" The answer is your pride. How much are you willing to humble yourself and be sincere, transparent, and honest with yourself?

Is it truly worth it? Only you can determine that. Do you want to continue battling with your children, or would you prefer to enjoy peace and harmony within your family? One thing is certain: peace of mind and spirit lead to joy, harmony, rest, and good health. In contrast, unresolved problems can lead to illness, stress, and even more serious consequences.

Carrying resentment and hatred is burdensome; it only weighs you down. It's far better to address issues openly and move forward with life. God has gifted us with wisdom and strength through His spirit to navigate our decisions. The choice is yours: continue deceiving yourself or embrace honesty and resolve issues in a constructive way.

So, how can you foster a sense of harmony and connection with your children?

1. Be Transparent: Make it a point to communicate openly with your children. Don't hide the truth behind lies, as this only complicates relationships. Honesty builds trust, and trust is foundational to any strong relationship.

2. Always Be Honest: Honesty should not be just an occasional act; it should be a way of life. It's crucial to embody honesty rather than merely speak it. Sometimes, the truth may lead to uncomfortable moments, but these moments are necessary for growth and understanding.

3. Practice Integrity: Living a life of integrity means your actions align with your words. Authenticity in your behavior fosters a safe space where your children feel valued and understood.

4. Encourage Open Dialogue: Create an environment where your children feel comfortable expressing their thoughts and feelings without fear of judgment. Encouraging their honesty will reinforce the importance of transparency in your relationship.
In the end, being sincere can only lead to positive outcomes. Sincerity does not harm anyone when it is rooted in justice and love. It's time to leave behind the masks and confront issues head-on, paving the way for healthier, more fulfilling relationships with your children.

Chapter 6

Dont talk, Listen to reason

My beloved brothers, I want you to understand this: all of you must be quick to listen, slow to speak, and slow to get angry.

James 1:19

Every child is born with the intrinsic ability to communicate, capable of expressing their feelings and thoughts. However, today's society is plagued by a significant communication gap that fosters insensitivity, ignorance, and difficult behavior among children. This issue can be traced back to a lack of effective communication, which is essential for emotional well-being and development. We express ourselves through various means, including speech, body language, and written words— all part of our fundamental human experience.

Unfortunately, many parents overlook their children's communication needs due to stress, time constraints, or other life challenges. This neglect can lead to severe consequences, such as insecurity, anxiety, depression, and even physical health problems. The failure to address a child's need to communicate can create a harmful cycle that negatively impacts their emotional state and overall well-being.

Today's children are growing up in a fast-paced world where they are exposed to a diversity of cultures and behaviors. While this can enhance their understanding and reasoning skills, it can also lead to personal frustration, especially in school environments filled with various influences. Conflicts arise as children navigate these complex social situations, often resulting in negative experiences such as bullying. Bullying has become a pervasive issue, exacerbated by the behavior of those who have not been taught respect and empathy.

The responsibility for this behavior often lies with the parents, who may fail to instill essential values in their children. The cycle of poor behavior is perpetuated when children engage in bullying or other disrespectful actions, not necessarily out of malice but due to their upbringing. This troubling trend can lead to devastating consequences, including severe mental health issues and even tragic outcomes.

It is crucial for parents to recognize the importance of fostering open lines of communication with their children. By attending to their emotional needs and encouraging expression, parents can help mitigate the negative effects of societal pressures and bullying. Ultimately, it is the responsibility of parents to create an environment where children feel safe to communicate, ensuring that they grow up with the confidence and tools necessary to navigate life's challenges.

When I was a child, I faced the harsh reality of bullying. I was born on November 18, 1996, but my arrival was delayed beyond the expected due date, leading my body to adapt in ways that made me different. Doctors and my mother were unsure why this happened, but the result was that my ears were slightly misshapen, a detail that set me apart from my peers.

In school and even at church, my appearance became a target for taunts. I was labeled with names like "Santa's Elf," "Dumbo," and "Troll Ears." These hurtful words cut deep into my self-esteem and emotional well-being, fostering resentment toward my own body. For a long time, I believed I was a mistake in this world simply because I didn't look like everyone else. The anxiety and despair that filled my childhood stemmed from constant rejection, making me feel unwelcome and unwanted.

Playing games often meant being the last one picked, a painful reminder that my physical appearance influenced how others perceived me. A few peers would glance at me with disdain, refusing my friendship based solely on how I looked. This led to years of feeling isolated and rejected, not only by classmates but also by those who were supposed to be allies, like teachers and church members. The bullying continued despite my attempts to seek help; my cries for it seemed to prompt only more mockery and ridicule.

I urge parents to be vigilant about their children's interactions. A child's emotional and psychological well-being can be damaged by the harsh treatment of their peers, whether at school or in other social settings. Discrimination and bullying are widespread, and it's essential to recognize that a child may be suffering trauma due to the insensitivity of those around them.

Children growing up with insecurities often feel worthless, losing sight of their value because of what others say. It's crucial for parents to instill strong values and principles in their children so they can stand up for themselves without inflicting pain on others. We must break the cycle of irresponsible parenting and promote kindness and respect among kids, creating a safer and more supportive environment for all.

REMEMBER:
A responsible father plays a crucial role in raising children who are respectful and well-mannered, instilling in them a sense of security and emotional well-being. It's essential for a father to be present and attentive, especially during the challenging times that children face.

Listening to a child's concerns and feelings is vital. When children reach out to share their struggles, it's important that their words are heard and valued. Genuine love is demonstrated through active listening; dismissing their thoughts or judging them can undermine their sense of worth and belonging within the family. Building a strong foundation based on open communication fosters a healthy relationship and empowers children to grow into confident individuals.

FREQUENTLY ASKED QUESTION:
How do I know if my child is experiencing be littling behaviors and depression in their life?

Answer: Children who experience hurtful behavior often carry the effects into their adult lives, manifesting signs that set them apart from others. Recognizing these signs is crucial, as they can indicate underlying issues such as depression and anxiety. Here are some common signs and symptoms to be aware of:

1. Persistent Sadness: A continual mood of sadness, anxiety, or a feeling of meaninglessness.

2.Changes in Sleeping Habits: Insomnia or oversleeping, disrupting normal rest patterns.

3.Appetite Changes. Either reduced appetite leading to weight loss or increased appetite resulting in weight gain.

4. Concerns and Worries: An overwhelming sense of worry about various aspects of life.

5. Irritability: Increased frustration or anger over minor issues.

6. Chronic Physical Symptoms: Ongoing pain or discomfort with no clear medical explanation, such as chronic pain or digestive issues.

7. Difficulty Concentrating: Challenges in school or work, including trouble remembering details or making decisions.

8. Fatigue: Persistent tiredness or lack of energy that doesn't improve with rest.

9. Feelings of Guilt: A pervasive sense of hopelessness, worthlessness, or self-blame.

10. Suicidal Thoughts: Any indication of thoughts about death or self-harm should be taken seriously.

11. Internal Tension: A sense of constant unease or tension.

12. Changes in Appetite: Similar to earlier, this can manifest as either loss of appetite or overeating.

13. Loss of Sexual Interest: In married or older children, a notable decline in interest in sexual activities.

14. Frequent Headaches or Migraines: Recurring headaches that can be symptomatic of stress.

15. Dizziness: Episodes of lightheadedness that may stem from anxiety.

16. Back Pain: Chronic back pain that does not have a clear physical cause.

17. Breathing Issues: Trouble breathing, often linked to anxiety or panic attacks.

18. Heart Problems: Palpitations or unexplained heart-related symptoms that can arise from emotional stress.

19. Gastrointestinal Disorders: Upset stomach or other digestive issues without clear medical reasons.

20. Abdominal Pain: Ongoing discomfort in the abdominal area.

21. Feelings of Unsafety: A consistent sense of being unsafe or threatened.

22. Social Isolation: Frequently being alone or preferring solitude over social interactions.

23. Lack of Co-habitation: Not living with others, which can heighten feelings of loneliness.

24. Difficulty Expressing Oneself: Stopping mid-conversation or struggling to share thoughts and feelings.

25. Quietness: A tendency to remain silent or withdrawn in social situations.

26. Slow Walking: Moving at a slow pace that conveys disappointment or anguish.

27. Rudeness in Defense: Being aggressive or disrespectful, often as a defense mechanism.

28. Disregard for Boundaries: Not respecting educational or personal limits set by authority figures.

29. Pityful Dressing Styles: Wearing dark or drab clothing that reflects their emotional state.

30. Haircuts That Hide the Face: Choosing styles that obscure facial features, often as a form of retreat.

31. Facial Expressions of Affliction: A countenance that suggests ongoing distress or suffering.

32. Extreme Body Modifications: Seeking out tattoos or piercings that may symbolize internal pain.

33. Listening to Depressive Music: A tendency to gravitate towards music that reflects or amplifies feelings of sadness.

34. Avoidance of Light: Blocking out natural light, indicating a desire to retreat from the outside world.

35. Social Withdrawal: Spending days locked away in their room without social interaction.

36. Messy Living Spaces: A disorganized environment that may reflect internal chaos.

37. Irresponsibility: A lack of organization in daily life or a disregard for responsibilities.

38. Dark Interests: Attraction to gothic or emo culture that aligns with feelings of despair.

39. Self-Harm Signs: Visible cuts or scars that signify coping mechanisms for emotional pain.

40. Interest in Dark Art: Drawing or engaging with art that depicts themes of death and darkness.

41. Casual Dress and Grooming Neglect: Opting for loose or unkempt clothing as a sign of low self-care.

42. Poor Hygiene: Neglecting personal cleanliness, possibly as a reflection of emotional state.

43. Interest in Substance Use: Seeking out drugs or alcohol as a method of escape from distress.

44. Party Culture Participation: Attending parties as a means to forget personal issues temporarily.

45. Alcohol as a Coping Mechanism: An ongoing interest in drinking and party culture.

46. General Substance Use: Smoking or experimenting with drugs as a means to cope.

47. Clubbing and Parties: Finding refuge in nightlife as a distraction from problems.

48. Exploration of Risky Behaviors: Engaging in high-risk activities or relationships.

ALL WITH THE PURPOSE OF"RELIEVING" THEIR PAIN.

A child who is emotionally hurt often exhibits a preference for either extreme isolation or overwhelming party environments. It's crucial for parents and caregivers to be aware of these signs, as they can provide insight into a child's emotional state.

1. Preference for Loneliness: If a child often chooses to be alone, avoids social interactions, or spends excessive time in their room, it may indicate feelings of sadness or anxiety. This desire for solitude could be a response to bullying or emotional distress, signaling that they are struggling to cope.

2. Attraction to Parties: Conversely, a child who frequently seeks out parties or social gatherings may be attempting to escape their feelings through distraction. They might believe that engaging in loud, chaotic environments can mask their pain or provide temporary relief from their internal struggles.

Both extremes are important to recognize. A child who isolates themselves may need encouragement and support to open up about their feelings, while one who constantly seeks social events might benefit from discussing their motivations for this behavior. Open communication, active listening, and a nurturing environment can help children feel safe expressing their emotions, allowing for healthier coping mechanisms and overall well-being. Monitoring these behaviors can lead to timely interventions and a stronger emotional foundation for your child.

Remember that the word of God says: *"The thief comes only to steal,kill and destroy..."(John 10:10).*

You must start working with your children's insecurities.The enemy is so cunning that he takes advantage of the absence of teaching to deceive your children into believing that you do not care about their well-being, their health and even their existence. He wants to steal their joy,their purity,kill their dreams and the illusions they have about life, destroy their moral and spiritual faith to make them believe that God does not exist and that they are alone,without purpose and destiny.
Do not allow the enemy to take advantage of your children's loneliness,teach them that they must learn to have an intimate relationship with God and that the problems they are going through in their lives are not for life,that the negative thoughts that come to their minds They are not necessarily for them to fulfill that thought.Teach them how to combat those thoughts.

FREQUENTLY ASKED QUESTION:
How can I teach my child to combat negative thoughts?

Answer:

Ephesians 6:13-17(NLT)
Put on all the pieces of the armor of God to be able to resist the enemy,in bad weather.Thus,after the battle,they will still stand firm. Stand your ground,putting on the belt of truth and the breastplate of God's justice.
Put on the peace that comes from the Good News as shoes so that you can be fully prepared.
Raise the shield of faith to stop the fiery arrows of the devil.
Put on salvation as a helmet
Take the sword of the Spirit,which is the Word of God.

YOUR CHILDREN NEED:

Learn to always be ready to combat the thoughts of the enemy with the word of God. Put on all the pieces of the armor of God to resist the enemy in times of evil. Understand that the struggles you face in your emotions are not merely about flesh and blood but involve spiritual forces that aim to cast a negative light on you. As stated, we do not fight against enemies of flesh and blood, but against evil rulers, authorities of the invisible world, powerful forces of this dark realm, and evil spirits from the heavenly places.

Speak the truth and defend it fairly to avoid doubts. The truth is more easily defended when the word of God is consistently practiced and scrutinized. Stand firm, putting on the belt of truth and the breastplate of God's justice. Learn to make decisions grounded in the Word of God so that the peace of God can abound in your life, ensuring you're always prepared. Wear the peace that comes from the Good News as your shoes.

Have conviction in your faith so that when challenges and negative thoughts arise, that faith can protect you against doubt, insecurity, and temptations, guiding you to make decisions aligned with the will of God rather than fleeting emotions. Raise the shield of faith to extinguish the fiery arrows of the devil.

Constantly reflect on your salvation, as this awareness helps prevent decisions that could jeopardize your personal faith and impacts your everyday life. Wear salvation as your helmet, keeping it at the forefront of your mind.

Make it a habit to read the Word of God regularly. When temptations or life's challenges arise, you'll be equipped to combat negative thoughts that may impede your ability to carry out God's will. Memorizing Scripture empowers you to make decisions rooted in God's Word instead of being swayed by fleeting emotions—take up the sword of the Spirit, which is the Word of God.

Additionally, prioritize communication with your children. While reconciliation is important, listening is equally crucial. Children often hesitate to share their problems with parents because they perceive a lack of attention or time. When they want to express feelings or confess something troubling, they might feel brushed aside because parents are preoccupied with daily tasks or distractions. It's essential to create a space where they feel heard and valued, ensuring that their thoughts and feelings are met with understanding and support.

This type of attitude from parents can cause depression, frustration, and a sense of helplessness in their children. They may find themselves asking, "What should I do? If my parents don't help or support me, if they seem uninterested or indifferent, what then?" When parents work hard but still scold their children for not meeting expectations, it fosters feelings of hopelessness. Children may start to lose trust in their parents and seek solutions and advice from others, including peers who might not have their best interests at heart.

It's crucial to remember that as a parent, you are responsible for protecting, caring for, teaching, guiding, and providing for your family. Providing isn't limited to financial support; it also encompasses giving love, understanding, affection, and your time. Sharing wisdom and knowledge is vital in helping children navigate their own paths.

Your children have their own needs, dreams, and goals, and they rely on your guidance to learn how to achieve them. If they don't receive that guidance from you, they may turn to others who may not have the right experience or intentions. Unfortunately, children often accept advice from those who may be in difficult situations themselves, leading to poor choices and misguided paths.

The consequences of parental irresponsibility can be heavy; they often lead to unnecessary burdens, sleepless nights, and regret. Listening to your children is essential. Take the time to sit down with them, build trust, and show them that you can be both a parent and a friend. Demonstrate that you're there to support them through both good times and bad, rather than judging or criticizing.

You're the superhero in their lives, the solution to their problems. By listening and understanding, without making them feel like they're the worst or shaming them for their mistakes, you can be the guiding force they need. Respect their rights as your children, provide them with knowledge and encouragement, and help them realize their potential. When they feel heard and supported, it paves the way for them to grow into successful individuals.

FREQUENTLY ASKED QUESTION:
How can I avoid damaging the communication between my children and I?

Answer:
How can I avoid damaging the communication between my children and me?

1. Listen First: Prioritize listening to what your children have to say before jumping in with responses. Sometimes they just need to express their thoughts and feelings.

2. Avoid Judgment: Don't judge their actions or decisions without understanding the full context. Listen to their reasons

for what happened and approach the situation with empathy.

3. Don't Rush to Conclusions: Take your time to hear everything your child wants to share. Make sure you have the complete picture before forming an opinion.

4. Show Compassion: Be compassionate and sensitive to your child's emotions. If they are upset and crying, offer a comforting hug and let them know you are there for them.

5. Empathize: Before giving advice, try to put yourself in their shoes. Understand that every child is different, and what worked for you may not be applicable to them.

6. Encourage Positivity: Offer words of encouragement that build their self-esteem and inspire them to believe in themselves. Your positive words can significantly impact their lives.

7. Unconditional Love: Love your children unconditionally, just as Christ loves you. Show them that they can always rely on your support and affection.

8. Reflect on Wisdom: Consider reading Proverbs 3:3-8, which emphasizes the importance of love, faithfulness, and the wisdom that comes from trusting in God.

Chapter 7

Taking care of Parental Influence

What a joy for those who do not follow the advice of the wicked, nor walk with sinners, nor do they associate with scoffers, but they delight in the law of the Lord, meditating on it day and night.

Psalms 1:1-2

A famous saying, "Tell me who you are with, and I will tell you who you are," highlights the profound impact that the people around us can have on our lives. This idea is echoed in the book of Proverbs, which emphasizes the importance of discerning the influences we allow into our lives, especially as parents. The people we choose to associate with can significantly shape our perspectives and the environment in which our children grow.

Children often mirror their parents' attitudes and values, making it crucial for parents to be selective about the company they keep. If parents surround themselves with individuals who demonstrate values like forgiveness, kindness, and excellence, it's likely that their children will adopt these same principles. Conversely, associating with those who lack responsibility or moral integrity can lead to detrimental influences on the entire family.

Parents should be wary of friendships with individuals who have difficulty maintaining healthy relationships or who engage in destructive behaviors. Friends who demonstrate poor parenting, lack discipline, or have unstable lifestyles can pose risks to the family unit. Aligning with such individuals may inadvertently lead to similar patterns within your own family.

If issues arise within your family life, it may be necessary to reevaluate and distance yourself from friendships that hinder your relationship with God, your partner, and your children. Although it can be tough to let go of friends who seem fun or make you laugh, remember that such influences can ultimately lead to spiritual decline and unrest in your home. Prioritizing your family's well-being over temporary enjoyment is essential. Seek friendships that uplift you, encourage growth, and embody the virtues you wish to instill in your children. These relationships should exemplify values aligned with the teachings of faith, and you should celebrate successes together, fostering an environment where your children feel cherished and proud of their family.
Children take pride in their parents, desiring to introduce them

without apprehension. It's vital to be the kind of parents that they can confidently present to others. These healthy role models can inspire your children to appreciate family harmony and uphold high standards, especially in their interactions with peers.

Finding friends who demonstrate good manners and principles will ultimately beneficiate your family's dynamic. As 1 Corinthians 15:33 warns, "Bad company corrupts good character," it is vital to surround yourself with those who can strengthen your family's values.

To maintain a positive family atmosphere, being willing to cut ties with unhelpful friendships is necessary. Good influences will bear good fruits in your life, while negative influences will lead to undesirable outcomes. The Psalmist captures this wisdom well:

"Blessed is the man who does not follow the counsel of the wicked, nor stay in the path of sinners, nor cultivate the friendship of blasphemers, but delights in the law of the Lord, and meditates on it day and night." (Psalm 1:1-2, NIV).

By rooting your friendships in goodness and righteousness, you position yourself and your family to thrive—much like a fruitful tree planted by the riverside. When you surround yourself with people who meditate on the Word of God, you will bear the fruit of a vibrant, flourishing life. Prioritize relationships that enrich your life and foster a sense of integrity and purpose for you and your children.

FREQUENTLY ASKED QUESTION:
How can I identify people who do not contribute anything good to my life and my family?

Answer:
The behaviors listed are serious concerns according to Galatians 5:19-21, which highlights various forms of negative conduct that can hinder our spiritual well-being. These include:

- Sexual immorality
- Impurity
- Sensual passions
- Idolatry
- Sorcery
- Hostility
- Strife
- Jealousy
- Outbursts of fury
- Selfish ambition
- Discord
- Division
- Envy
- Drunkenness
- Unbridled parties and similar sins

These actions can indeed create relational and spiritual discord, which threatens the health of our communities and family lives. It's a reminder for us to carefully consider our choices and the company we keep. By pursuing a life grounded in love, respect, and kindness, we can foster healthier relationships and align our lives with God's teachings. The warning is clear: "Anyone who lives that kind of life will not inherit the kingdom of God." This serves as a strong caution against surrounding ourselves with individuals who embody these negative traits. For the sake of your family's well-being, your marriage, and your children, it's important to distance yourself from those who may jeopardize the good that God has provided you through His mercy and grace. Cherish and protect the blessings in your life, and be intentional about the influences you allow in.

Proverbs 6:16-19 highlights certain characteristics that are not only harmful but deeply despised by God. These include:
- Arrogant eyes
- A lying tongue
- Hands that kill the innocent
- A heart that plots evil
- Feet that run to do evil

- A false witness who breathes lies
- One who sows discord in a family

These traits are often contagious, spreading negativity and discord within our communities and relationships. Therefore, it's crucial to be mindful of the company we keep. Surrounding ourselves with individuals who embody these characteristics can lead to a toxic environment.

To nurture positive relationships and promote a healthy life for ourselves and our families, we must filter our friendships. Choose to engage with those who uplift and inspire you, rather than those who may lead you down a harmful path. Remember, the influence of our friends can greatly impact our values and actions, so be intentional about who you allow into your life.

FREQUENTLY ASKED QUESTION:
What are the characteristics of people who *do* contribute to my spiritual life,my family and my children?

Answer: Galatians 5:22-23
The characteristics of individuals who positively contribute to our lives include:
- Love
- Happiness
- Peace
- Patience
- Kindness
- Goodness
- Fidelity
- Modesty
- Self-control

People who embody these qualities align with the teachings of God and show obedience to His word. Such friendships are invaluable; they guide us to stay on the path of Christ, supporting us in our journey of faith and helping us remain anchored in the truth of God's love.
Surrounding ourselves with those who inspire us to be more

like Christ is essential. These influences encourage us to refine our character and personality, fostering personal growth day by day until we reach our fullest potential.

Positive influences not only motivate us but also strengthen our family relationships. They teach us to heal from past wounds and to let go of negative experiences, helping us create a nurturing and loving environment for ourselves and our children. By intentionally choosing to connect with those who uplift us, we can build a supportive network that enriches our lives and aligns with our values.

Chapter 8

The Art of Patience

Those who have understanding do not lose
their temper; Those who are easily
angered show great foolishness.

Proverbs 14:29

The word *art* means: capacity,ability to do something.

The word patience means:the ability to suffer or endure something without getting upset.

Each parent must learn to exercise their ability to endure difficult situations without getting upset. After the Crucifixion and the Resurrection, Jesus stayed for 40 days teaching and speaking with His disciples about the last things He needed to communicate. One of the significant statements He made before ascending to Heaven is found in Acts 1:8, where He said: "But you will receive power when the Holy Spirit comes upon you; and you will be my witnesses, telling people about me everywhere: in Jerusalem, throughout Judea, in Samaria, and to the farthest places of the earth" (NLT).

The word "power" signifies having the ability or capability to do something efficiently and with ease, time, or place. Every parent has the ability to exercise patience in everything they set out to do. It's important to recognize that patience is not an inherent gift. Rather, it is cultivated over time and through experiences.

The apostle Paul, in Galatians 5:22-23, elaborates on the fruits of the Holy Spirit, stating: "Instead, the kind of fruit that the Holy Spirit produces in our lives is: love, joy, peace, patience, gentleness, kindness, faithfulness, humility, and self-control" (NLT). This means that if a follower of Jesus has the Holy Spirit, they must embody two crucial qualities: patience and self-control. These are not skills acquired through magic words or purchased; they are the fruits born from a life in constant relationship with God, enriched by the Holy Spirit within.

FREQUENT PRAYER:
"God,give me patience!"

STOP!
We do not have to ask God for patience, as patience is part of the package when God gives us His Spirit to dwell within us.

Patience is a vital tool that God knows we will utilize in our lives to exercise self-control. In essence, if there is no self-control, there can't be true patience, and vice versa. These two qualities go hand in hand.

It's important to recognize that many people make the mistake of praying for attributes that do not need to be specifically requested but rather developed over time. By nurturing our relationship with God and allowing His Spirit to work in us, we can cultivate the self-control and patience.

FREQUENTLY ASKED QUESTION:
How can I develop patience?

Answer:
"If you are wise and understand the ways of God,demonstrate it by living an honest life and doing good deeds with the humility that comes from wisdom;But if you have bitter envy and selfish ambitions in your heart,do not cover up the truth with boasting and lies.For envy and selfishness are not part of the wisdom that comes from God.These things are earthly,purely human and demonic.For where there is envy and selfish ambition,there will also be disorder and all kinds of evil."James 3:13

Patience occurs when the quality of a person changes. It is developed when an individual experiences transformation, which is why the presence of the Holy Spirit is essential. The Holy Spirit is the one who changes our hearts and purifies our intentions. Without this divine influence, we may find ourselves manifesting the fruits of the flesh, as outlined in Galatians 5:19-21: "The fruits of the flesh are: sexual immorality, impurity, sensual passions, idolatry, witchcraft, hostility, quarreling, jealousy, outbursts of rage, selfish ambition, discord, divisions, envy, drunkenness, riotous parties, and other similar sins."

As Johann W. Von Goethe stated, "What you feed within you is what grows." This highlights the importance of nurturing our inner selves with the right influences and focusing on spiritual growth. By allowing the Holy Spirit to guide us, we cultivate qualities like patience and self-control, leading to a more fulfilling spiritual life.

Your abilities will develop depending on what you feed,if you want to be impatient,feed the meat,if you want to be patient feeds the spirit.You cannot change if you feed both things at the same time,you must decide which one you are going to dedicate your time,attention,effort and energy to,if you try to do both things at the same time what you will get for doing it is a big headache and You will feel lost as if you were in a sea with no escape.This will lead you to depression,anxiety,frustration and will damage your emotional,mental,physical and spiritual health.

Do not do it!
The way you can change is by soaking up knowledge with spiritual direction.If you are filled with the Spirit,you live and walk in the spirit.Your steps,thoughts,decisions and ambitions will be firm,and the margin of error will be smaller.Otherwise,if you decide to take the side of the flesh,setbacks,an emotional void,wrong decisions,constant mistakes and damaging ambitions await you.You cannot make mistakes that harm you,you need habits and advice that will lead you to change the person you are and eventually set you on the path to success.

"If you are wise and understand the ways of God,show it by living an honest life and doing good deeds with the humility that comes from wisdom..."Galatians 5:19(NLT)

What every follower of Jesus must implement in their life is the constant practice of living an honest life by doing good works. This approach fosters a transformation in one's ambitions, leading to a shift in focus, actions, words, thoughts, vision, dreams, goals, and everything that shapes our personality.

Following the Ten Commandments of the ancient law serves to align our flesh with the preferences and conditions of the spirit. The flesh will never naturally desire to comply with what the

Spirit of God wants to accomplish. Therefore, the flesh must be guided to submit to the spirit's instructions. By doing so, we can effect a change in our attitude, which is fundamentally what self-control is about.

Self-control goes beyond merely refraining from good or bad actions; it involves managing and directing our actions, words, will, conscience, and understanding so that they align with the Word of God. This is why Jesus stated, "When the Spirit of truth comes, He will guide you into all truth. He will not speak on his own account, but He will tell you what He has heard and tell you what will happen in the future" (John 16:13, NLT). By embracing this guidance, we can navigate our lives with greater clarity and purpose, allowing the Holy Spirit to influence our every aspect positively.

The Holy Spirit guides us in various important ways, enabling us to:
- Stop and consider our words before we say them
- Think twice before speaking or taking action
- Evaluate the good and bad before making decisions
- Pause to reflect on the consequences of our actions
- Avoid acting impulsively
- Steer clear of deliberately offending others
- Become better followers of Jesus
- Serve as examples for those who do not yet know Jesus

These qualities reflect the characteristics and fruits of someone who exercises self-control in their life. This is why Peter encourages us by saying, "In view of all this, do your best to respond to the promises of God by complementing your faith with an abundant supply of moral excellence; moral excellence with knowledge; knowledge with self-control; self-control with perseverance; perseverance with submission to God; submission to God with brotherly affection; and brotherly affection with love for all. The more you grow in this way, the more productive and useful you will be in the knowledge of our Lord Jesus Christ" (2 Peter 1:4-8, NLT).
By embracing these principles, we cultivate a deeper

relationship with God and become more impactful witnesses in our communities, demonstrating the transformative power of the Holy Spirit in our lives.

FREQUENTLY ASKED QUESTION:
How can I change my mindset using the Holy Spirit?
Answer:
"Do not imitate the behaviors or customs of this world,but rather let God transform you into new people by changing your way of thinking.Then you will learn to know the will of God for you,which is good,acceptable and perfect."Romans 12:2
To leave the customs of the world we must do what Jesus said:*"If any of you want to be my follower,you must abandon your own way of life,take up your cross and follow me."Matthew 16:24(NLT)*

First, we must let go of the way the world lives. It is challenging to align ourselves with the will of God while still holding onto worldly habits. To truly embrace a life in Christ, we need to adopt new customs and practices that develop over time in God's presence. This calls for a total separation from the world and a commitment to living a new and fulfilling life grounded in God's grace and mercy.

The only way God can work in us is when we cleanse our lives of everything that has intoxicated us—habits, beliefs, traditions, and mindsets that keep us trapped in despair. This also requires distancing ourselves from those who influence or incite us to act against our own values and convictions. As the Word reminds us, *"This means that everyone who belongs to Christ has become a new person. The old life has passed away; a new life has begun" (2 Corinthians 5:17, NLT).*

Embracing this transformation allows us to step into a life that reflects God's will and purpose, empowering us to live authentically and fully as new creations in Christ.

Talking about a new life involves changing habits, beliefs, traditions, mentalities, and friendships. You cannot enhance your quality as a person if you are not willing to let go of what curses you. God has countless blessings in store for your life, your family, and especially for your children. Don't squander the opportunity to transform your life, uplift your children, and strengthen your marriage—it's truly worth everything!

Transforming your thoughts from the flesh to the Spirit is the most effective path for your life. Consider these changes:
- Choosing thoughts that honor God is transformative.
- Making decisions that honor God brings real change.
- Leaving behind secular traditions reshapes your life.
- Involving God in all aspects of your life leads to growth.
- Changing habits, work ethics, traditions, and customs fosters improvement.

Denying yourself means rejecting what curses you—those things that hinder your personal progress. Changing your life is not easy; it is far from a bed of roses. In fact, it can be one of the most challenging endeavors because it goes against our carnal nature. The desires, ambitions, dreams, and goals we pursue from our perspective often seem more appealing than those aligned with God's Spirit. Yet, it is within this struggle that we must choose whether to pursue God's will or to satisfy our fleshly inclinations.

It is essential to cultivate habits that nurture the Spirit in order for it to grow. The less we engage in carnal exercises, the more our spirits can flourish. We must weaken the flesh so that the spirit can thrive abundantly. The more we consume spiritual nourishment, the greater our spiritual strength will become. Embracing this journey of transformation leads us to a more fulfilling and purposeful life in accordance with God's design.

IMPORTANT POINTS:

To exercise patience, a transformation is required within you. You must allow God to change you so that your way of thinking evolves. It's essential to nourish your soul with spiritual food rather than relying on carnal sustenance. Leaving behind worldly customs and habits is crucial. Denying yourself and following Jesus will help you become a positive influence in your children's lives.

Consider these reflective questions:
- What current habits do you need to change in your life?

- Which people are acting as stumbling blocks, preventing you from moving forward?

- What steps can you take to improve your habits?

- What attitudes, actions, or gestures does your child exhibit that test your patience?

- How have you reacted to your child in those moments?

When faced with impatient moments, adopting healthy habits can make a difference. Here are some questions to guide you:

Ask:

- What is happening in this situation?

- Why is he or she reacting that way?

- Why do I react like this?

- Who or what caused this reaction?

- When will I stop responding this way?

- How can I help my child navigate this?

Hear:

- Listen without passing judgment or condemnation.

- Consider the reasons behind their reactions before responding.

- Take a moment to think through anything you have to say before reacting.

- Be aware of physical signs, such as your breathing and the volume or quality of your voice.

- Collaborate with your child to work toward a solution.

Inquire:

- Who or what caused the problem?

- What is the root of this issue?

- Is there a viable solution?

- What are the pros and cons of various possible decisions?

- Which personal areas are impacting the emotional, mental,

spiritual, or soulful aspects of the situation?

Sorting through these questions can not only help you develop patience but also strengthen the bond you have with your child, creating a nurturing environment for both of you to grow. In every situation, it is crucial to identify the root of each problem. Without this identification, it becomes difficult to resolve issues and remove obstacles. As parents, we must act like a surgeon during a heart transplant, thinking quickly and making right decisions to avoid losing the patient. A surgeon may have time on their hands, but they remain calm, clear-headed, and prepared, having absorbed the necessary knowledge to navigate obstacles effectively.

As a parent, you should strive to maintain the same calmness as a surgeon in challenging situations. While the task is daunting and requires considerable effort, it can ultimately save a life. This is why it's essential to prepare your spiritual and mental intellect. You need to respond with composure during difficult moments, equipping yourself with the right words, actions, decisions, and outcomes. A wrong step can lead to the emotional and spiritual distress of a child.

It's important to remember that young people do not always think logically when they are upset. Often, during their moments of anger, they will react impulsively, saying the first thing that comes to mind. Therefore, you must be prepared to respond in a way that doesn't escalate the situation or further hurt their emotions. Learning to communicate without causing offense is key.

Every parent should also cultivate the skill to respond effectively, much like a boxer. Julio César Chávez, a legendary boxer known for his resilience and skill, prepared diligently, maintained discipline, and showed remarkable courage in the ring. He understood how to defend himself while effectively countering his opponents. His relentless effort and preparedness allowed him to maintain an impressive record, inspiring future generations.

As a parent, you must similarly soak your mind in knowledge and strategies that help you manage family conflicts effectively. Always be prepared for whatever challenges arise, so you can offer solutions to those who may be struggling with the situation.

Remember that you and your partner hold authority within your family. Decisions made together can dramatically impact your children's lives, whether positively or negatively. It's vital to ensure that your parenting is aligned and mutual, promoting a healthy environment for your children's growth.

When encountering difficult situations with your children, think carefully about the potential consequences of your words before you speak. This mindful approach can save you from misunderstandings and unnecessary conflicts. God has equipped you as a parent to guide your children in a healthy and productive manner, so don't let the misguided advice of others sway you. Instead, seek to hear God's voice and direction.

The Bible offers wisdom on communication: "A gentle response turns away anger, but harsh words inflame tempers" (Proverbs 15:1, NLT). This suggests the importance of responding calmly and thoughtfully, rather than reacting out of anger or frustration.

Chávez stood out in boxing not just for his physical ability but for his composure under pressure. He demonstrated that true strength comes from maintaining a level head and responding with skill rather than engaging in verbal conflict. Similarly, as a father, you must analyze the situation before reacting. Avoid thoughts like, "This is my house, and I'm in charge" or "What I say goes here." Such mentalities often stem from insecurity and can lead to repeated mistakes that cultivate resentment among your children.

Don't allow yourself to cultivate negative emotions within your family. Instead, become a wise gardener who roots out harmful thoughts and behaviors. Be a responsible leader who plans for the future, properly tending to the emotional landscape of your children's lives.
Misfortunes often occur as a domino effect, arising not from fate or divine intervention but from a lack of caution in actions and words towards your family. James reminds us, "When you are tempted, remember not to say, 'God is tempting me.' God is never tempted to do evil, and he never tempts anyone" (James 1:13, NLT). It's crucial to recognize that temptation arises from our own desires, which can lead to sinful actions.

If you seek wisdom, remember to ask God for guidance; He promises to give generously to those who ask without rebuke, provided your faith remains strong (James 1:5-6). By maintaining focus on God's direction and being proactive in your parenting, you can foster an environment where both you and your children thrive.

FREQUENTLY ASKED QUESTION:
How can I solve a fast problem using patience?

Answer: James 1:2
Dear brothers, When you are faced with any problems, consider it an opportunity for joy, because you know that the testing of your faith develops perseverance. Let this perseverance finish its work so that you may be mature and complete, lacking

nothing. — James 1:2-4 (NLT)

Unhealthy habits can emerge during impatient moments. For instance, screaming desperately into the wind might seem like a way to express oneself, but it often signals a lack of self-control, sanity, and respect for those around you—especially family, children, and partners. It's more beneficial to express anger, frustration, or fury in private, where your feelings won't negatively affect others, allowing for freedom of expression without limits.

Frustration should never be displayed in front of children, as these reactions can inflict psychological trauma. Such expressions can create insecurity, low self-esteem, and even lead to physical health issues like anemia, high blood pressure, and other ailments. Children are incredibly perceptive; they absorb the emotional cues from their parents—facial expressions, body language, and even words spoken can have lasting impacts.

Reacting physically out of anger is another grave mistake a parent can make. Hitting or mistreating children is never justified and is against both God's teachings and the law. Such actions can leave deep scars, and children may struggle to forgive their parents. It may require professional help from trained ministers or psychologists to address the emotional trauma inflicted. It's crucial for parents to seek assistance themselves if they find they are struggling to control their anger.

James further reminds us that "envy and selfishness are not part of the wisdom that comes from God" (James 3:12-16, NLT). The act of abusing children is rooted in selfishness, as it neglects the fact that every human being has feelings and deserves respect. Taking out one's anger on a child is a cowardly act. As human beings, we are called to be better than mere instinctual reactions like animals.

A follower of Jesus should not engage in violence toward

others—be they children, colleagues, or acquaintances. We must strive for a life distinct in its discipline and connection to Christ, avoiding hypocritical double standards.

Sadly, many who attend church come from backgrounds where such violent customs persist, with parents justifying their actions. It's disheartening to learn that even leaders of faith may engage in abusive practices, perpetuating a cycle of harm and causing children to shy away from the church.

Ephesians 6:4 (NLT) tells us not to provoke our children but to nurture them with the teachings of the Lord. No child who faces physical abuse can feel happy or accept "corrections" with good intentions. Each instance of mistreatment breeds resentment and anger.

Instead, we should take inspiration from God's compassionate nature. He communicates with us through various means, urging us to correct our paths with love and mercy. Let us strive to embody that same approach in our parenting and interactions with others.

FREQUENTLY ASKED QUESTION:

Is it love,patience and mercy to hit your children with fists when they stress a parent?

Answer:
The answer is no; hitting your children in response to stress is not an act of love, patience, or mercy. On the contrary, it is a manifestation of selfishness and pride, indicating a lack of peace in the heart and the absence of God's presence within the individual.

Children who experience this form of abuse from their parents face a myriad of detrimental effects, including:
- Low self-esteem: Repeated acts of violence can lead children to feel worthless and unlovable.
- Insecurity: They may struggle to feel safe, both physically and

emotionally.
- Mental boundaries: They establish protective walls that can hinder healthy emotional connections.
- Fear: Constant exposure to a volatile environment can make them wary of relationships, fearing that love may come with conditions or violence.
- Loss of confidence: They may doubt their abilities and feel incapable of navigating the world around them.
- Anxiety: The stress of living in a fearful environment can lead to chronic anxiety.
- Emotional and physical stress: The toll on their mental health can manifest in physical ailments as well.

It's crucial for parents who have made the mistake of resorting to violence to understand the repercussions this behavior can have on their children. Acknowledging the harm caused is the first step towards healing. They must learn how to address and rectify the damage done to prevent further harm to themselves and their children.

Children living in homes where abuse occurs may feel a persistent sense of fear and anxiety. They become hyper-vigilant, constantly worried about when the next episode of violence might arise. Their reactions can vary by age:

- Preschool Children: Young children who witness domestic violence may regress to earlier behaviors, such as bedwetting or thumb-sucking. They may cry more frequently, have trouble sleeping, show signs of terror, or experience severe separation anxiety.

- Tweenagers: Children in this age bracket often internalize guilt and might blame themselves for the violence. Their self-esteem takes a hit, leading to disengagement from school activities, poor grades, fewer friendships, and increased behavioral issues. They may also develop physical symptoms like headaches and stomachaches due to the stress.

- Teenagers: Teens who witness abuse might act out through

negative behaviors, such as fighting with family members or skipping school. They may engage in risky behaviors—like substance abuse or unprotected sex—develop low self-esteem, and find it challenging to form friendships. Teenage boys who have experienced childhood abuse are more likely to act aggressively, while girls may withdraw and face depression. Understanding the profound impact of domestic violence on children is essential for fostering healthier environments. Healing and restoration begin with awareness, education, and a commitment to change.

FREQUENTLY ASKED QUESTION:
What are the long-term effects of domestic violence or child abuse?

Answer:
More than 15 million children in the United States live in homes where domestic violence has occurred at least once. This alarming statistic highlights the potential long-term effects on these children, who are at greater risk of repeating the cycle of violence as adults. Research indicates that children who witness domestic abuse are at a significantly increased risk of becoming involved in abusive relationships themselves or perpetrating abuse.

For instance, a child who observes his mother being abused is ten times more likely to become an abuser in his own relationships as an adult. Similarly, a girl raised in a home where her father abuses her mother is six times more likely to experience sexual abuse than a girl who grows up in a non-violent environment.

The consequences of exposure to domestic violence extend beyond immediate emotional and psychological harm. Children who witness or experience emotional, physical, or sexual abuse are at a higher risk for various health problems as they grow into adulthood. These may include:

- **Mental Health Issues:** Many struggle with conditions such as depression and anxiety as a result of their traumatic experiences.

- Physical Health Conditions: Adult survivors of childhood abuse may face chronic health problems, including diabetes, obesity, and heart disease.

- Low Self-Esteem: The impact of childhood trauma often manifests in low self-worth, further complicating relationships and overall life satisfaction.

The cycle of abuse can continue through generations if not addressed. It is crucial for society to recognize these patterns and provide support systems aimed at breaking the cycle. Resources such as counseling, education, and intervention programs are essential for helping these children heal and forge healthier relationships in the future. By promoting awareness and proactive measures, we can help mitigate the long-term effects of domestic violence on children.

FREQUENTLY ASKED QUESTION:

Can children recover from seeing or experiencing domestic violence or abuse?

Answer:

Yes, children can recover from witnessing or experiencing domestic violence or abuse, but recovery varies significantly from child to child. Each individual responds differently to trauma; some may exhibit greater resilience, while others may be more sensitive to the impacts of their experiences. The success of recovery depends on several key factors, including:
- A good support system: Having a network of supportive family members, friends, and professionals can greatly enhance a child's ability to heal. When children feel understood and protected, they are better positioned to process their experiences.

- Healthy relationships with trusted adults: Positive interactions with nurturing and trustworthy adults can provide children with reassurance and guidance. These relationships are crucial for developing a sense of safety and stability.

- High self-esteem: A child's confidence and self-worth play a significant role in their ability to recover. Building self-esteem through encouragement and positive reinforcement can help children feel empowered and capable of overcoming their past experiences.

While some children may not completely forget the trauma they witnessed or endured, they can still learn healthy coping mechanisms to manage their emotions and memories as they grow older. The earlier a child receives assistance—whether through counseling, therapy, or supportive community resources—the higher their chances of becoming healthy, mentally sound adults.

Overall, with appropriate support and intervention, children can find pathways to recovery and lead fulfilling lives despite their past experiences. It's essential to prioritize their healing journey and provide the necessary tools for coping and resilience.

FREQUENTLY ASKED QUESTION:

How can I help my child heal after seeing or experiencing domestic violence?

Answer:

You can support your children in their recovery from witnessing or experiencing domestic violence in several meaningful ways:
1. Help Them Feel Safe: It's essential for children to feel secure. Consider whether leaving the abusive relationship would enhance their sense of safety. Discuss the importance of healthy relationships with your child to reinforce this understanding.

2. Talk About Their Fears: Encourage open dialogue where your child can express their fears. Reassure them that the violence is not their fault, nor is it yours. Learning how to communicate about domestic violence effectively is crucial.

3. Discuss Healthy Relationships: Help your child learn from their experiences by identifying what constitutes healthy relationships versus unhealthy ones. This dialogue will equip them with the knowledge they need as they enter into their own relationships in the future.

4. Educate About Boundaries: Teach your child that no one— be it family members, teachers, coaches, or authority figures— has the right to make them feel uncomfortable or to touch them without consent. Additionally, help them understand that they must respect others' boundaries as well.

5. Establish a Reliable Support System: Beyond parental support, seek out school counselors, therapists, or other trusted adults who can provide ongoing assistance. Be aware that school counselors are mandated to report signs of domestic violence or abuse.

5. Seek Professional Help: Cognitive Behavioral Therapy (CBT) can be particularly effective for children who have experienced trauma. This type of therapy helps children reframe negative thoughts into positive ones and learn healthy coping strategies for stress. Consult your doctor for a recommendation of mental health professionals experienced in youth trauma. Many domestic violence shelters and organizations also provide support groups specifically for children, allowing them to connect with peers who understand their experiences.

6. Personal Change: The most significant factor in recovery is the parent's commitment to changing unhealthy patterns into positive, constructive habits. By doing so, you help your child cultivate a sense of emotional stability and security. Remember, children often mirror their parents' behaviors; your process of change will foster their healing.

Remember:
- To exercise patience, personal change is essential.
- Allow God to transform your mindset for the better.
- Feed your spirit with uplifting, spiritual nourishment rather than negative influences.
- Distance yourself from detrimental worldly customs.
- Embrace self-denial and follow Jesus as an example for your children.
Healthy Habits to Implement:
- Ask before acting: Consider your responses carefully and thoughtfully.
- Listen before commenting: Give your child the space to express themselves fully before jumping in with your thoughts.
- Investigate to understand the root of issues: Take the time to understand what is truly going on.
- Find solutions: Strive to address problems constructively, avoiding exacerbation of existing issues.

By following these principles and strategies, you can create a nurturing environment that promotes healing and resilience in your children, helping them thrive despite their past experiences.

COMPILATION OF SICK HABITS

- Scream desperately into the wind
- Physically hitting with fists and slaps
-*Make permanent decisions,with temporary emotions*

Enthusiasm without knowledge is worthless;haste produces errors Proverbs 19:2(NLT)

These habits and behaviors must be addressed at their core to foster meaningful change. Bad habits and erroneous actions often stem from inadequate parental education. It may come as a surprise, but we frequently hear about moral education without recognizing how differently it is applied.

The apostle James specifically highlighted the power of the

tongue, implying that our words can bring both life and death. Decisions we make are declarations that should be carefully thought out, as our choices influence those we care about deeply. As a parent, you hold a vital role—your decisions shape not only your life but also the perceptions and futures of your children.

For instance:
- Exemplary parenting sets a standard that children tend to follow.
- Harsh parenting can lead children to feel distant and lacking warmth in their relationship with you.
- A loving, affectionate approach cultivates trust, security, and respect, as parents meet their children's emotional needs.
- In contrast, strictness without love breeds insecurity and low self-esteem, pushing children to hide their true selves and seek temporary relief in unhealthy ways, such as substance abuse.
Many toxic patterns have persisted across generations, with some parents reacting impulsively or through anger. While we often hear phrases like, "Respect your elders," or reminders to use polite language, there are subtle messages that can harm rather than help. These messages can lead to bad habits forming within children.

Parents must not be selective in applying values; instead, they should remember the importance of consistency and encouragement. Establishing an environment of open communication and unconditional love is essential. By modeling positive behavior, reinforcing respect, and fostering emotional support, parents can break the cycle of negativity and raise healthier, more confident children.

A CHRISTIAN,WITH BAD HABITS,IS A FATHER WITH BAD HABITS.

Before becoming good parents, it is essential to first be good Christians, as a life grounded in transparency reflects a strong foundation. A wise and sound decision-making process is crucial to being a good father. This begins with being aware of your actions and avoiding the trap of making permanent decisions based on temporary emotions.

The Word of God warns us in Jeremiah 17:9 (NLT), "*The human heart is the most deceitful thing there is, and extremely perverse.*" As parents, it's vital not to be swayed by fleeting emotions because they can lead you astray. History offers examples, such as Cain, whose emotional turmoil drove him to commit the irreversible act of killing his brother, resulting in a curse for himself and his descendants.

Absalom also allowed his emotions to dictate his actions, leading to the horrific betrayal and division of his family, culminating in tragedy. Similarly, Judas Iscariot let his emotions cloud his judgment, ultimately betraying Jesus for thirty silver coins, leading to a bitter end.

Every decision carries consequences, whether positive or negative. It's essential to harness this understanding and not allow feelings of frustration, anger, depression, or anxiety to drive your choices. As Proverbs 14:29 (NLT) states, *"Those who have understanding don;t lose their temper; those who are easily angered show great foolishness."*

Emotions can be overwhelming, but it's vital to remain disciplined and thoughtful. By prioritizing your spiritual journey and making wise decisions, you can provide a stable and loving environment for your children to thrive.

FREQUENTLY ASKED QUESTION:

What habits can I practice to avoid getting angry easily or acting out towards my children?

Answer:

- Respect What Your Child Communicates: It's vital to listen and respect what your child shares with you. If they express a truth that resonates with you, avoid reacting with anger or hurtful words. Understand that their honesty may stem from a place of frustration and a desire for change. Accepting their truths is a sign of maturity, and it can open the door for meaningful conversations.

- Analyze the Situation Before Speaking or Acting: Always take a moment to think before responding. Avoid impulsively reacting to your child's actions; instead, allow your mind to process the situation. This pause can help you respond more thoughtfully.

- Avoid Shouting: Responding to tense situations with shouting only escalates the conflict. Remember Proverbs 15:1 (NLT): "A gentle response turns away anger, but harsh words inflame tempers." Strive for calmness in your approach, as it can diffuse tension and encourage an open dialogue.
- Never Argue About Who Is Better: It's crucial to avoid competitive conversations about who is better or more accomplished. Such comparisons can create insecurity and emotional imbalance, leading to emotional detachment. Instead of competing, celebrate each other's achievements. Your focus should be on uplifting one another with words of encouragement. This fosters security, emotional balance, respect, and love within your family.

Fighting with your children over achievements or who earns more is not worth it. Adopting a mindset similar to that of a Spartan soldier means being disciplined and focused on support, understanding, and growth rather than pride and competition. Nurturing a loving environment encourages your children to flourish and feel valued for who they are.

ALWAYS REMEMBER:
"Your best ally in times of combat is the man who is on your side..."King Leonidas(Movie 300)

Chapter 9

Productive Parents,
Productive Children

The wise are cautious and avoid danger;
Fools, confident in themselves, rush in
recklessly.

Proverbs 14:16

On many occasions, you hear parents complain about their children because of their behavior, their clothing choices, or even their way of thinking. But have you ever asked yourself, "What have parents done to avoid collateral damage?" That is, what steps have they taken to prevent their children from acting or thinking in certain ways? It's crucial to recognize that children often embody the significance their parents place on them and the actions and reactions they demonstrate.

Every parent should be aware of these factors, especially since it is common for them to overlook the importance of maintaining a close connection due to fatigue or instinct. It's frequent to hear older children express sentiments like, "My dad made the mistake of not enforcing the same discipline with my siblings as he did with me." As the eldest of six siblings, I've echoed similar thoughts. Conversations with various parents, including my own, reveal that this topic rarely sparks consistent dialogue. Instead, it tends to be discussed in passing, without any real exploration of solutions or alternatives for the issues at hand—issues impacting countless families.

When parents are questioned about this, you might hear remarks like:
"The older you get, the more you relax your standards."
"It's just too overwhelming to deal with everything the same way."
"It's not the same; when you're older, you simply want to rest without having to confront the changing attitudes and behaviors of children during their puberty."

For every parent who does not have more than 1-2 children I say:

If you are not willing to be responsible with more children when you are 35 or 40 years old, do not have them. Instead of being a contribution, they will be a burden for you, for your siblings at home, and for society. This is because, due to a lack of education, discipline, and parental effort, negative and non-productive children are being reproduced.

For every parent who has more than 2 children I say:
Do not stop trying to keep your children, as they say in Mexico, "in line." You might find it tiring or difficult to deal with their attitudes and behavior, but it is up to you whether you want to take care of your grandchildren alone in your old age or if you want to be responsible for your children as well. If you want to ensure that your grandchildren are a joy rather than a burden, invest time and dedication into raising your children to be responsible and good people who contribute to your life, society, and to their own future families.

If you choose not to educate your children, to give them everything they want without discipline, and let them do as they please, you may find yourself caring for not just your grandchildren but your children as well. The Bible reminds us: "Discipline your children, and they will give you peace of mind and gladden your heart." (Proverbs 29:17 NLT).

The real issue today is the lack of parental education, often due to parents who themselves lacked proper discipline and guidance. This is not strictly the fault of changing educational systems, the government, or teachers. The main reason children lack proper education is because parents have been, and continue to be, irresponsible in their roles as educators.

The government's role is to maintain order in society, while teachers are responsible for imparting knowledge in areas like literature, mathematics, science, and history. Neighbors and community members can choose to live their lives as they wish and share their experiences if they want to.

However, the primary responsibility of parents is to instill moral values and principles in their children—discipline, responsibility, proper conduct, thinking, self-control, and character development. This ensures they grow up to be contributing members of society rather than burdens to others. Ultimately, you must take responsibility for your children because no one else can love them and care for them like you do. True parental love is demonstrated through education, not through material gifts, money, or luxuries, but through discipline, time, and guidance. The Bible states, "Those who do not use the rod of discipline hate their children. Those who truly love their children care enough to discipline them." (Proverbs 13:24 NLT)

A rod is a straight branch from a tree, and its purpose is to straighten anything that is not aligned. The rod mentioned in the Bible can be applied in various ways, including verbal and physical methods. It's important for parents to discern when to use each approach.

The physical rod is a traditional method used to correct or punish someone for disobedience or wrongdoing. It serves to instill awareness in children or individuals who fail to comprehend the consequences of their actions. When a child refuses to understand the reasoning behind a rule or correction, physical discipline may sometimes be necessary. God has incorporated the concept of pain into our human experience to help us learn about life. Pain can act as a wake-up call, prompting reflection and understanding when happiness alone does not lead to correction.

When God calls attention to our behavior and we fail to respond, He permits situations in our lives that may cause discomfort, guiding us toward conscience, repentance, and reconciliation. While using the physical rod can be painful, it is often effective in bringing about correction.

On the other hand, the verbal rod serves as a more passive method aimed at avoiding physical punishment. However, it requires more effort and patience to implement effectively. Unlike the immediate impact of physical discipline, verbal guidance can take longer to yield results, depending on the severity of the situation. When employed correctly, the verbal approach encourages reflection and understanding over time, fostering lasting behavior change.

THE PHYSICAL WAND IS NOT ALWAYS EFFECTIVE

It is essential for every parent to recognize that the physical rod is not always effective on its own; discipline is a complex formula composed of various components. Understanding these components is crucial for ensuring that correction leads to genuine spiritual and psychological growth in children.

If you approach discipline without a clear purpose, you may inadvertently harm your children, potentially leading to significant repercussions in their future. A lack of direction in discipline can result in struggles as they seek to find their identity and understand their place in the world. Therefore, parents must strive to create a balanced approach that combines different methods of discipline, focusing not only on correction but also on guidance and support. This holistic strategy can help children develop into well-rounded individuals who are aware of their values and responsibilities.

FREQUENTLY ASKED QUESTION:

What is the secret formula of purposeful discipline?

Answer:

First, it's crucial to understand that the formula for effective discipline cannot work unless parents first change their way of thinking. As a parent, it's important to realize that you are the primary example for your children. If you don't align your life with the values you wish to instill—such as character, self-control, behavior, language, your relationship with God, and biblical knowledge—your children may feel justified in questioning your authority. They might say, "What are you telling me? First, fix your own life."

It's common for parents to want to guide their children without first addressing their own shortcomings, but it doesn't work that way. For discipline to be effective, you need to be in a good place yourself. Setting an example and making changes in your own life is vital because it establishes authority. Your children will be more inclined to respect your words if they see you living by the principles you teach. If you lack that alignment, they may not believe, obey, or take your guidance seriously. Therefore, don't waste your breath if you haven't established your authority first through your actions and example.

SECRET FORMULA:

The first ingredient of the secret formula for purposeful discipline is faith. Faith provides us with the certainty and conviction regarding what we believe, even when we cannot see it (Hebrews 11). To implement purposeful discipline, you must believe in God and His Word; by doing so, you can follow the divine instructions provided.

Purposeful discipline involves adhering to a pattern that you believe in—not simply because someone shared their experiences, but because God's Word offers correction, guidance, and perfection. Your children should be disciplined not because a pastor said, "hit them," or a grandmother advised, "punish them with the rod." Instead, discipline should arise from your desire to educate and guide your children toward a better life. This approach will ultimately bring rest to your life and peace to your soul.

The second vital ingredient in purposeful discipline is communication. It is essential for your children to understand why they are being corrected. If they don't grasp the reasons behind the discipline—if they just associate it with punishment—they may harbor resentment in their hearts. Conversely, a child who knows why they are being corrected will accumulate wisdom. As the Word of God says, "The rod and correction give wisdom."

A common mistake many parents make is disciplining through physical punishment without providing corrective guidance. Some might say, "I hit my children so they learn to respect," or "I hit them so they understand." This approach reflects a misunderstanding that can persist for generations. It's crucial to remember that children are not animals to be chased around or treated harshly; they are human beings entrusted to you by God, with the authority to correct and nurture.

You must exercise your parental authority and remember that you hold authority in your home. You have the power to decree actions and desires within your household. It's necessary to learn how to communicate words of authority and establish laws that govern your home, providing your children with a solid foundation of understanding and conscience.

FREQUENTLY ASKED QUESTION:

How can I establish laws and rules so that my children raise awareness?

Answer:

You must establish clear rules and laws so that your children understand what they can or should do, as well as what they should not do. Setting laws creates a framework that helps keep children on the right path (Proverbs 22:6, Hebrews 12:13). It's crucial that you don't express weakness through your words or actions; showing character and keeping your promises is essential.

Many parents unintentionally use weak and challenging language, saying things like, "I am going to hit you," or "You're going to see, your dad/mom is going to hit you," or "Do it again, and you'll find out." Such statements challenge children to test boundaries instead of providing them with clear warnings. Over time, this can negatively affect their understanding of authority. When children are confronted by legal consequences later in life, they may view those laws as challenges rather than as boundaries.

For this reason, it's important for household rules to mirror government laws—sharp, consistent, and enforced. This approach instills a sense of seriousness, ensuring that children grasp that your words carry weight and are not to be taken lightly. You should replace weak threats with decisive actions.

If you say you are going to punish your child, follow through with it—don't just threaten. If you need to impose a consequence, do so firmly and consistently. Do not just threaten to take away privileges or devices; take them away if necessary. If you plan to cancel outings, follow through on that action.

Your words and actions should convey authority, differing significantly from weak or uncertain language. Your tone should be as unwavering as a hot comal ready to warm tortillas. Your words must be firm and consistent. For example, if you tell a child, "Don't touch it because it's hot, and you could get burned," they may touch it anyway but will learn from the consequence that follows.

Your character should reflect consistency with your words and actions. Be gentle and compassionate in your heart, but firm and resolute in your discipline. It's important to separate your emotions from your character when exercising authority.

If your child does something wrong, discipline them, but also take the time to explain why their actions were inappropriate. Help them understand the consequences—both positive and negative—of their behavior. Always communicate clearly with them so that they receive knowledge and understand that the discipline is a result of their actions. This way, they can recognize that the moment of pain was a direct consequence of their choices, and it served a purpose. Never administer punishment without an explanation; always take the time to talk with them.

EXAMPLE:

because I was a very naughty, disobedient, and argumentative child. He seemed to handle everything with everything. Older people who knew me say that I even kicked the church ushers, spat on them, and hit them with a closed fist. I behaved badly because I was naturally curious; everything intrigued me, and I always wanted to know and experience new things.

I still remember drinking the juice and eating the cookies that were supposed to be used for the Holy Supper. I was just a child and didn't understand their significance. To me, they were just delicious snacks. It wasn't until I grew older that I realized what I did was inappropriate since those items were meant for a special occasion at church.

My father had a specific way of disciplining my brothers and me. He would often take us to a room, sit down to be at our eye level, and talk to us face-to-face. He would ask, "Do you know why I'm going to hit you?" and we would respond, "Yes," explaining why we deserved to be punished. After that, he would ask us to turn around, and then he would hit us with a belt three times.

Once he was done, he would either continue talking to us, offering words of correction, or give us some space to calm down. Sometimes he made us stand in the corner to think about what we had done. After a while, he would return, sit down again, and discuss the situation with us, explaining why the punishment was necessary and insisting we learn from our mistakes.

He would always end with hugs and prayer, asking God to grant us wisdom, understanding, and to help avoid any feelings of bitterness or resentment. Instead of leaving us angry, he wanted us to feel at peace and to understand why we needed to behave better. Afterward, we would go to our mother for another hug, and we'd move on with our day, feeling calm and enlightened.

I can genuinely say I'm thankful for my father's approach to correction. It instilled wisdom and understanding in me, helping me grow into a good person. I appreciate his strong character, his firmness, and consistency, which taught me to be a good son and now a good adult and child of God.

FREQUENTLY ASKED QUESTION:

How can I correct my children when they are older?

Answer/Example:

When children grow up and enter their teenage years, the discipline system must evolve. In their younger years, physical discipline might have been used due to their lack of understanding and consciousness. However, for children aged thirteen and older, the approach should shift to be more peaceful and tolerant, as they are now capable of comprehension and have the ability to respond to conversations and criticisms.

As parents, it's important to realize that the old methods of punishment aren't effective anymore. Instead, we need to embrace a more thoughtful approach that hinges on logic, wisdom, and open communication. With their education and maturity, adolescents are equipped to reason, engage in dialogue, and defend themselves against accusations, whether they're unfounded or valid. It's crucial to avoid making accusations based on assumptions, gossip, or lies since this can harm the relationship and cause emotional distance.

Before addressing your child, remember that responsible parenting involves:
1. Raising and educating children to be respectful individuals.
2. Building security and confidence within them.
3. Listening to them during the toughest moments.
4. Paying attention to their words and feelings when they are trying to share something important.

Effective discipline for a young person demands that you employ the patience of an elephant, the insight of an owl, and the gentleness of a bird. Listening and observing should take precedence over speaking, as teenagers often grapple with insecurities and past trauma. It's essential for parents to cultivate an environment of trust so that their children feel secure in confiding in them.

FREQUENTLY ASKED QUESTION:

Creating a strong bond of connection with your children is essential for earning their trust. Here are some effective ways to foster that connection:

1. Keep Personal Struggles Private: Avoid sharing your own insecurities, traumas, or past mistakes with your children. This allows them to view you as a source of strength and stability.

2. Avoid Public Embarrassment: Never embarrass your child in public for their actions. Instead, address issues privately to maintain their dignity and self-esteem.

3. Show Unconditional Support: Be their ally and educator rather than an attacker. Your consistent support will help them feel safe and valued.

4. Be Present: Make an effort to be there for them during times they feel alone. Your presence can make a significant difference in their emotional state.

5. Check In Regularly: Send messages or make phone calls to ask how they are doing or how they feel. This shows you are thinking of them and care about their well-being.

6. Provide Affection: Offer hugs, kisses, and gentle words of encouragement unexpectedly. These gestures remind them of your love and support.

7. Focus on Teaching, Not Punishing: When they make mistakes, guide them on how to avoid repeating them instead of scolding. A teaching approach is more beneficial than a punitive one.

8. Be Patient with Their Growth: Understand that changes take time, and be patient as they navigate through their experiences.

9. Help Them in Hard Times: Support them through tough patches, even if they haven't treated you well. Demonstrating compassion can teach them valuable lessons about love and forgiveness.

10. Follow the Golden Rule: "Do not repay evil for evil. Don't respond with insults when people insult you. Instead, respond with a blessing" (1 Peter 3:9). This mindset fosters a positive environment.

11. Embrace Parental Discipline: Educating adolescents requires more discipline than during their younger years. Be a guiding force, embodying love, compassion, understanding, and humility.

12. Avoid Provoking Frustration: As mentioned in Colossians 3:21, avoid irritating your children with words or actions that offend them. Aim to offer good advice and appropriate support to help them navigate their challenges.

By integrating these practices into your parenting, you'll cultivate a deeper sense of trust and connection with your children, making it easier for them to confide in you as they grow.

FREQUENTLY ASKED QUESTION:

How can I be a productive parent with my children?

Answer:
The term "productive" in Latin refers to having the capacity to carry out or create something, encompassing meanings like efficacy, virtue, profitability, usefulness, fruitfulness, convenience, viability, and effectiveness. To "engender" means to cause or bring about.

As a father, you must embody the qualities of a potter. Imagine taking a lump of clay and placing it on a wheel. As you turn the wheel, you provide constant attention, shaping the clay into a glass, plate, vase, or flower pot. The potter understands that if they divert their focus, the clay can easily lose form or quality. Likewise, a father must remain vigilant and engaged to guide his children toward becoming useful and productive individuals.

Being a productive father requires dedicating time, attention, teaching, correction, discipline, and building character. This is not an easy task—it demands commitment and effort. It's important not to allow laziness to take over. Instead, actively teach, instruct, correct, and guide your children, fostering their gifts and abilities. Your role is to help them grow into individuals who contribute positively to the world around them, ensuring they are productive rather than destructive. Embrace this responsibility fully, as it has a profound impact on their future and the lives they touch.

FREQUENTLY ASKED QUESTION:

What are my responsibilities as a parent to raise productive children?

Answer:

Teach them to:
Teach your children the following valuable principles to help them grow into well-rounded individuals:
1. Fear God: Instill a deep reverence and respect for God.
2. Be good workers: Encourage a strong work ethic in all they do.
3. Have values: Teach them about integrity, honesty, and morality.
4. Full faith in God: Foster a trusting relationship with God and belief in His plans.
5. Respect others: Cultivate empathy, kindness, and respect for all individuals.

6. Discipline: Instill the importance of self-control and following rules.

7. Responsibility: Teach them to take ownership of their actions and decisions.

8. Financial management: Instruct them on saving, investing, and avoiding impulsive spending.

9. Seek God's purpose: Encourage them to pray and seek guidance on their calling in life.

10. Develop gifts: Motivate them to explore and diversify their talents.

11. Compassion: Teach them to be loving, caring, and humane.

12. Respect laws: Instill respect for both earthly laws and God's commandments.

13. Win souls: Encourage sharing their faith with others.

14. Love God: Inspire them to love God wholeheartedly.

15. Appreciate what they have: Teach gratitude for both big and small blessings.

16. Interpersonal skills: Encourage them to interact positively with others.

17. Release fears: Help them understand and let go of their fears.

18. Overcome trauma: Support them in facing and healing from personal traumas.

19. Value wisdom: Emphasize the importance of seeking wisdom in their lives.

20. Be humble and meek: Teach them about humility and gentleness.

21. Study the Bible: Encourage careful and understanding reading of the scriptures.

22. Consequences of disobedience: Teach about both positive and negative repercussions of straying from God's will.

23. Self-management: Instruct on how to manage their personal domain and responsibilities.

24. Understanding sexuality: Educate them on God's views regarding sexuality.

25. Preparing for marriage: Share knowledge on what it takes to develop a healthy marriage.

26. Hearers and doers: Teach them to not only listen but also act on God's Word.

27. Adapt to environments: Help them learn how to behave appropriately in different contexts.
28. Read building books: Encourage reading materials that stimulate growth and development.
29. Daily lessons: Share valuable life lessons to promote reflection and understanding.
30. Musical skills: If possible, teach them to play an instrument.
31. Sports: Encourage participation in sports they are passionate about.
32. Communication: Foster their ability to communicate effectively.
33. Confidence: Encourage self-assurance and belief in themselves.
34. Family support: Teach them to support family members through various situations.
35. Organization: Instill the importance of being organized and avoiding debt.
36. Banking skills: Teach them how to open, maintain, and manage a bank account.
37. Tax knowledge: Educate them on basic tax responsibilities.
38. Entrepreneurship: Encourage entrepreneurial thinking and skills.
39. Life skills: Teach them how to survive challenging situations.
40. Domestic skills: Instruct them in cooking, cleaning, and maintaining a household.
41. Clothing care: Teach them about laundry, ironing, and personal grooming.
42. Decision-making: Help them learn to make wise decisions.
43. Friendship choices: Teach them to discern good and bad friendships.
44. Avoid substance abuse: Educate them on the dangers of drugs and peer pressure.
45. Physical health: Encourage regular exercise and healthy eating habits.
46. Curiosity: Reinforce the importance of asking questions when they need knowledge.
47. Sibling care: Teach them to be caring and protective of their siblings.

48. Understanding loyalty: Explain the importance of being loyal and supportive.
49. Tithing and offering: Teach the benefits of giving back financially.
50. Housework knowledge: Ensure they understand household tasks to prepare for adulthood.
51. Work ethic: Encourage diligence over laziness.
52. Daily routines: Promote waking up and sleeping at consistent times.
53. Ministry involvement: Teach them how to serve a ministry in church.
54. Prayer and fasting: Highlight the importance of these spiritual practices.
55. Personal grooming: Teach how to properly maintain hygiene and appearance.
56. Driving skills: Educate them on driving safely and responsibly.
57. Using tools: Promote skill in using various work tools.
58. Outdoor skills: Teach fishing and hunting as applicable.
59. Communication with God: Encourage expressing insecurities and concerns to God.
60. Moral discernment: Help them understand the difference between good and evil.
61. Spiritual growth: Teach how to grow spiritually and develop a relationship with God.
62. Discernment: Equip them to discern between lies and truth.
63. Negotiation skills: Teach them how to negotiate in various situations.
64. Talent development: Encourage refining and developing their God-given talents.
65. Writing and creativity: Foster skills in writing and drawing.
66. Holy Spirit's role: Explain the importance of the Holy Spirit in their lives.
67. Baptism and speaking in tongues: Teach the significance of these practices.
68. Relationship with God: Encourage establishing a strong, personal relationship with God.
69. Avoiding religion: Help them engage in true evangelism rather than mere religious practice.

70. Faithful discipleship: Teach them how to follow Jesus faithfully and share His teachings.
71. Swimming: Ensure they know how to swim, especially in deep water.
72. Basic construction skills: Provide knowledge on building a house.
73. Animal care: Teach them how to care for pets and maintain their well-being.
74. Legal awareness: Educate them on how to avoid legal issues.
75. Public speaking: Encourage skills in singing and speaking in public venues.
76. Craft skills: Teach them how to create various crafts.
77. Equality in respect: Emphasize treating everyone with equal respect.
78. Gardening skills: Teach them about planting, harvesting, and caring for plants.
79. Machine operation: Educate them on how to safely operate various machines.
80. Culinary skills: Encourage them to prepare special meals.
81. Knowledge sharing: Promote the importance of sharing knowledge with others.
82. Public etiquette: Teach them how to behave in public places, including restroom etiquette.
83. Self-sufficiency: Encourage being a help to others rather than a burden.
84. Life success: Instill principles that promote success in life.

By instilling these lessons and principles, you will help your children grow into accomplished, responsible, and compassionate individuals who can navigate life effectively.

As parents we have the responsibility to train and instruct our children in the best possible way,so that they are people who contribute to society,their family,and their spiritual life.
Educated children are not born,they are made!

FREQUENT EXCUSE:

My son doesn't want to!

STOP!
Tell me a verse where God says,"Ask your child if he wants to be productive in life." In none!
God specifically said

INSTRUCT,CORRECT,AND DISCIPLINE!

If your child doesn't want to listen to the instruction you give him,correct him.If your child doesn't want to change,discipline him with actions not words.He is not in them whether they want it or not,they are under the instruction,correction of your coverage,God backs your word and decree.

RECOMMENDED DISCIPLINES:
If your child doesn't want to stop being disrespectful, take away his benefits.
If your child doesn't want to study, remove everything that hinders him from getting good grades.
If your child doesn't want to stop using the phone, take it away.
If your child doesn't want to stop playing video games and locks himself inside all day, you should remove them.
If your child doesn't want to wash the dishes, there are no benefits.
If your child doesn't want to help around the house, let them know they will lose benefits.
If your child does not want to obey, let him know that there will be consequences.
If your child does not want to be responsible, do not benefit him with anything.

In conclusion, if your child does not want to follow your word and instructions, remove from him what is hindering him from fulfilling his duties as a child. Children are not going to die because you take away what has them hooked or addicted. They were born without devices and benefits and will be able to live without them. An educated and disciplined child is better than a neglected and forgotten child. An educated and disciplined son will never beg in life. A neglected and forgotten son will always beg for his daily bread.

Chapter 10

The Importance of Communication

Parents, do not exasperate your children, so that they do not become discouraged.

Colossians 3:21

"Be understanding of the faults of others and forgive anyone who offends you. Remember that the Lord forgave you, so you must forgive others. Above all, clothe yourselves in love, which unites us all in perfect harmony. And may the peace that comes from Christ rule in your hearts. For, as members of the same body, you are called to live in peace. And always be grateful." - Colossians 3:13-15 (NLT)

One of the fundamental exercises in the growth and development of each person on this planet is the ability to speak and exchange words. Everyone begins by learning to pronounce words and others to understand their meaning. Words are crucial in our daily lives; they help us achieve what we desire and what we want to remove from our existence.

Words are a combination of syllables, whistles, and a set of muscular efforts of the tongue that allow sounds to be heard from our mouths. God, the most important character in our existence, created communication as the primary tool to do and undo, to create and finish. When God said, "Let there be light," there was light. When He said, "Multiply," the earth multiplied.

God maintains a close relationship with His creation and His children. From the very first day to the present, there has not been a single day when God does not engage in the exercise of words. He uses them to lead, teach, guide, train, create, and even complete. This serves as a clear example of how vital communication is.

Even the Bible says: "Pray without ceasing." This means: never stop communicating the necessary words; never withhold words that could impact someone's life—or even your own. Words were made to be expressed through teaching, discipline, guidance, inspiration, and creation. It's essential to recognize that words must be utilized for their intended purpose—fixing problems, forgiving, and seeking forgiveness.

Every parent and child must understand that words are the fundamental key to preventing traumatic situations and protecting hearts and emotions. Words are necessary to navigate family issues—not mere expressions of faces or gestures, not money or material possessions.

Santiago, in his letter in chapter three, explains the immense power and magnitude of words; they can bring life or death, construction or destruction, peace or restlessness. Words are powerful, and it's vital to learn how to use them effectively.

Some parents mistakenly believe that communication is optional, but it's essential. Children cannot learn without communication, which fosters wisdom, knowledge, and experience. If parents overlook this, they may face a long, painful, and uncomfortable journey. Communication is the number one priority in the family. Without it, there can be conflict, lack of direction, and ineffective learning.

Parents must communicate about what is missing, what offends, what hurts, and what troubles them. A father, in particular, has the responsibility to correct, teach, guide, and direct his children. The true value of a father shines when he openly addresses problems with his kids. When fathers take the initiative to resolve differences, regardless of being right or wrong, it fosters respect, admiration, and love from their children. This is why I emphasize the importance of using words wisely.

Phase 1
RECOGNIZING THE ERROR
Sometimes, parents and children have arguments due to family differences, an action, a moment of displeasure, an uncalculated reaction, or simply a moment of frustration. What many fail to recognize is the importance of identifying the errors made during these discussions. Each family member must learn how to acknowledge their mistakes.
Often, tensions arise during transitional periods in a child's life —such as moving into adolescence or young adulthood. As the

world advances, children grow and gain experience and knowledge. Parents need to understand that their children need support and guidance, and it's neither fair nor productive to dismiss their voices by saying things like:
- "You don't have to tell me what to do."
- "You are no one to teach me."
- "I am your father," or "I am your mother."
- "This is my house, and what I say goes."
- "I pay the bills, so I decide how things are done."
These phrases can be harmful and undermine communication. Many parents mistakenly try to assert superiority in these moments, which can destroy a child's self-esteem, personal security, and trust in their parents.

A father doesn't need to prove his strength, position, or capacity to cause harm. Children want a father who protects them, listens to them, and encourages them—someone who shows unconditional support. It's crucial for fathers to understand that they shouldn't threaten their children with their strength, finances, or temperament.

Children are not wild animals without understanding. A father is not like a wild beast that needs to roar or show aggression to assert dominance. Instead, fathers are human beings equipped with the rational ability to make decisions wisely and with self-control.

James tells us, *"If you are wise and understand the ways of God, show it by living an honest life and doing good deeds with the humility that comes from wisdom. But if you harbor bitter envy and selfish ambitions in your hearts, do not boast about it or deny the truth. Such wisdom does not come down from heaven but is earthly, unspiritual, and demonic." (James 3:13-15, NLT)*

The Proverbs further state, "Scoundrels create problems; his words are a destructive fire." (Proverbs 16:27, NLT) This highlights the importance of being a good human being before trying to be a good father. To be a complete father, one must rectify personal attitudes and actions that harm their children. Pride, arrogance, and ignorance should be left behind for the sake of the children.

A loving father is ready to give everything for his children. True love inspires change, not imposition. God, the ultimate example of a perfect father, gave up His glory and life for humanity out of love. If God can set aside His majesty for us, what more can we do as human fathers to set aside our pride? Admitting mistakes as a parent is vital. It's crucial to understand that unresolved errors can have serious consequences for children. Words, actions, gestures, thoughts, and impulses all play significant roles in family dynamics.

Parents should not justify their irresponsibility just because they hold the title of 'parent.' Untreated wounds can lead to lasting effects on children, including depression, anxiety, and various psychological issues stemming from a lack of communication. It's essential to address these damages, ensuring that children are not left to deal with the fallout of a parent's actions.

Remember that, ultimately, God holds parents accountable for how they manage their families. Children are an invaluable gift from God, worth more than any material possession. By taking responsibility for your actions and words, the healing process can begin for both you and your children.

"It is better to be patient than powerful; it is better to have self-control than to conquer a city." (Proverbs 16:32, NLT) Let's strive for patience and understanding in our families for healthier relationships.

FREQUENTLY ASKED QUESTION:
What's the point of acknowledging my mistakes if my children don't change?
Answer:
The Word of God instructs every believer to declare and believe in things that are not as if they were. This means that

when faced with new challenges and opportunities for personal growth, you must embrace them, even if the potential for success seems minuscule. Never allow negativity to take root as you embark on your personal journey. By seeking the reasons to improve, you find motivation not just to please God but also to uplift your family and those around you.

Faith, in this context, is like a bouquet of roses to God; it captivates Him and brings Him joy. It can be said that faith drives Him wild because it represents action taken outside the realm of worldly logic. A person with stable reasoning might think, "With a materialistic mindset, success is unlikely." However, in the world of God, having faith and acting without reliance on logic is not madness—it's courage! God admires and rewards those who dare to break free from conventional reasoning to expect extraordinary outcomes.

Doing things by faith, even when current circumstances may not offer much hope, can indeed be challenging but it is far from impossible. Take the example of Abraham, whose faith was tested by God's instructions. Many fail to see that Abraham, at first glance, did not possess the qualifications needed for such a calling. He lived with his parents, was dependent, lacked children, and was not of Jewish descent; he was a pagan worshiping other gods. Yet, his faith was what shifted God's perspective.

The Bible tells us, "By faith, Abraham was justified and called the father of nations." Despite lacking qualifications or apparent reasons, it was Abraham's faith that forged a deep relationship with God. It was through that faith that he became a father at the age of 100 and laid the foundation for the twelve tribes, ultimately giving rise to the nation of Israel.

You may feel that your children give you little reason to change your personality, mentality, or beliefs, but remember that God alone is sufficient motivation for personal improvement. It's natural to feel hesitant about investing time to work on your ego, arrogance, and character. However, every good deed we perform on Earth will be rewarded, both here and in heaven. Do not expect applause from your children as you begin your transformation; this phase can often be the toughest, as the people we love most are often those who might discourage us. Don't rely on their validation; instead, seek God's approval.

Your partner could either hinder your growth or become your greatest ally; regardless, maintain your trust in God and keep pushing forward in your transformation process. Initially, your children may not notice the changes you're making and may even view your commitment skeptically, thinking it's as fleeting as a weight-loss journey.

Stay the course—whatever they may say—dismiss negative comments and intentional provocations. With time, your children will witness the fruits of your perseverance. They will experience them, embrace them, and as a family, you will glorify God through your examples of lifestyle, obedience, and testimony.

Admitting your mistakes will earn you respect. There is no child who doesn't admire a parent who humbly acknowledges their wrongdoing, saying things like, "Forgive me for my mistakes," or "I didn't meet your expectations."

A staggering 99.9% of parents who practice humility and recognize their faults often build healthy, mature relationships with their children. A balanced relationship ensures that no one feels superior or inferior; everyone is valued equally, receiving the same love, respect, and honesty. This mutual respect forms the backbone of trust between parents and children.

On the flip side, a father who is proud and arrogant is unlikely to earn genuine love and admiration from his children. Instead, he may breed resentment and rejection, as a lack of humility prevents him from owning up to his faults.

You have the power to decide the type of emotional garden you want to cultivate within your family. If you're inclined to maintain strife, then pride, arrogance, and stubbornness will prevail—but the fruits of that tree will only yield loneliness and despair. It would be wiser to uproot that tree, make firewood from it, and instead, plant a robust and flourishing tree filled with respect, humility, love, and wisdom.

The fruits of this new tree will bring delight, and living in harmony will offer peace and refuge, even in adversity.
"Be understanding of the faults of others and forgive anyone who offends you. Remember that the Lord forgave you, so you must forgive others. Above all, clothe yourselves in love, which unites us all in perfect harmony. And may the peace that comes from Christ rule in your hearts. For, as members of the same body, you are called to live in peace. And always be grateful." - Colossians 3:13-15 (NLT)

Phase 2
APPLYING FORGIVENESS
Living a Christian lifestyle requires constant self-correction in our character, behavior, thoughts, and way of living. In messages delivered by pastors during services, we often hear about the importance of forgiveness—specifically, that we should forgive those who have wronged us. However, one question many children have is: Why can't my parents apologize to me?

A significant issue, both historically and today, is the frequent arguments between parents and children, often without any reconciliation afterward. Leaving disputes unresolved can foster feelings of bitterness, hatred, and resentment. It's unwise to have arguments with your children and then walk away without resolution. This is one of the many mistakes a father (or parent) can make that negatively impacts the future of their children and their relationship with them.

Parents must learn to be humble rather than prideful, compassionate instead of judgmental, sincere rather than deceitful. Those parents who refuse to set aside their pride and acknowledge their mistakes risk losing touch with their children, sometimes completely.

Jesus said, "If you forgive those who sin against you, your heavenly Father will forgive you; but if you refuse to forgive others, your Father will not forgive your sins." (Matthew 6:14-15, NLT). This highlights the crucial role of forgiveness in family dynamics.

One of the most detrimental situations a family can face is heated arguments that go unresolved. Many parents and children display attitudes of arrogance, often thinking, "If they don't ask for forgiveness, I won't either," or "I'm the parent; I don't need to apologize," or conversely, "I'm the child; they should apologize to me." Such thoughts stem from a heart filled with pride and arrogance.

As a family, it's vital to understand that neither party is inherently worthy of forgiveness. No one on this earth is beyond error; we are all sinners with our own faults and failures. Forgiveness is not something we grant because it's deserved; rather, it's given out of grace for the benefit of both parties. Children often think they deserve forgiveness for their misbehavior, just as parents may expect the same; however, before the cross, it is ultimately God who determines who deserves forgiveness.

Jesus reaffirms this by saying, "If you forgive those who sin against you, your heavenly Father will forgive you; but if you refuse to forgive others, your Father will not forgive your sins." (Matthew 6:14-15, NLT). This means that if we seek God's forgiveness for our sins, both children and parents must practice humility and forgiveness towards one another. Only through this mutual forgiveness can we expect God to forgive our wrongs against Him.

Without forgiveness, there is no reconciliation. If we do not resolve conflicts on Earth, we cannot expect such resolution from Heaven. Forgiveness and repentance must be cultivated among family members to reap the rewards of God's grace. If we fail to practice forgiveness, we hinder God's ability to forgive our transgressions. The path to healing and restoration lies in our willingness to forgive one another.

FREQUENTLY ASKED QUESTION:

Why do I have to apologize to my son?

Answer:

Asking a child for forgiveness is not the easiest task for a parent, but it is undoubtedly one of the healthiest things you can do. It's akin to applying antiseptic to a wound; dealing with the hurt early on prevents complications like infection, which can lead to deeper issues down the line.

Forgiveness—both asking for it and offering it—is a commandment from Jesus, intended for both those who offend and those who have been wronged. Acknowledging your mistakes, whether it's due to bad attitudes, moments of anger, or hurtful words and actions, is vital for the emotional, spiritual, and psychological well-being of your child.

Here are some reasons why you should apologize to your child:
1. Obedience to God: God commands us to forgive one another as a way to be forgiven by Him.
2. Preserving Love: It protects the loving relationship you have with your child. Without it, they may feel unloved or even think you harbor resentment towards them.
3. Preventing Bitterness: By asking for forgiveness, you can help prevent your child from developing seeds of bitterness and hatred, not just towards you, but towards God as well.
4. It's Right Before God: Acknowledging your faults is an act of righteousness in the eyes of the Lord.
5. Counteracting Pride: Love is not self-serving; it does not seek to elevate oneself above others.
6. Guiding Your Child: An apology can be a guiding light, keeping your child from potentially straying down a destructive path.
7. Maintaining Harmony: Apologizing promotes peace and active harmony within the family unit.

8. Expressing Love: For your child, receiving an apology signifies that they are valued and loved, reinforcing their sense of belonging.

9. Building Trust: It fosters a relationship built on trust, encouraging open dialogue where they feel comfortable seeking your advice.

10. Valuable Gifts: Asking for forgiveness is a precious gift for a child, akin to giving them an expensive and heartfelt present that signifies your deep care for them.

Avoiding apologies can be detrimental; it breeds toxicity and harms children's emotional health. Children exposed to a lack of humility may hesitate to express their feelings, leading to self-doubt and insecurity. The sooner you seek forgiveness, the quicker the healing and growth can occur.

A child might distance themselves from faith simply because a parent, who claims to embody the Holy Spirit, fails to let go of their pride and arrogance. A loving father shows love and forgiveness, not hatred and resentment. Children thrive on their parents' expressions of compassion; the absence of such emotions can feel bitter and unwanted.

Living with rejection and indifference is a heavy burden for a child. They may prefer to withdraw than engage with parents who radiate negativity and resentment. God desires for both you and your children to live in freedom, filled with joy—not in captivity to pride and arrogance. No one should feel unappreciated, insecure, or suffer from low self-esteem.

Forgiving and seeking forgiveness brings liberation—for you and your child. Embrace this freedom and foster a healthier family dynamic!

FREQUENTLY ASKED QUESTION:

How can I apologize to my son?

Answer:

The rhetorical question often posed is: "What should you not do when asking for forgiveness?" Many parents struggle with this process, often failing due to a lack of understanding and self-reflection. Some attempt to make amends through gifts, money, or brief, insincere apologies, mistakenly thinking that these material gestures can replace genuine emotional healing. However, it's crucial for parents to recognize that financial gifts cannot mend wounds inflicted by hurtful words or actions.

To truly heal a wound of this nature, what is needed are words of wisdom—pure, sincere, and heartfelt expressions of regret. Countless children feel abandoned and empty when their parents equate forgiveness with material offerings instead of meaningful words. Many yearn to hear an apology from their parents, a longing so strong that it drives them to seek fulfillment in unhealthy ways, such as substance abuse, in an attempt to fill the void created by a lack of forgiveness.

As a parent, it's vital to understand that your child won't heal by receiving cars or video game consoles; real healing happens when you say, "Son, forgive me for offending you and for saying things that were wrong." When you earnestly apologize, your child will likely pause and listen intently to your words, because they need emotional and psychological support just as much as they need material things.

When approaching your child, you should do so with an attitude of honesty and good intentions. Understand that your child may react impulsively, possibly shouting or exhibiting anger in response to your apology. These are natural reactions, stemming from feelings of neglect and a deep-seated desire for recognition and forgiveness.

Children who are hurt often react in various ways—silence, indifference, anger, or even aggression—depending on the depth of their wounds. Be prepared for whatever reaction they may have, always keeping your own calmness and serenity at the forefront. While you might think their reactions are immature, it's essential to acknowledge that their feelings are valid.

When approaching the conversation, be mindful of your words and actions. Maintain a healthy mindset, as reacting with anger could further exacerbate the situation, re-opening emotional wounds. When children feel hurt, they often experience a sense of helplessness, which can drastically affect family dynamics and relationships.

Helplessness makes children feel unheard and ignored, creating a barrier of respect or an imposition of authority that can be damaging. When parents assert that they are in charge without allowing for open communication, children may begin to perceive themselves as slaves rather than as valued family members.

You must understand the difference between raising a child and raising a slave. A child who feels loved and valued will wish to remain with their parents, while a child who feels oppressed may resent their parents, finding it difficult to express their true feelings.

Ask yourself: How are you raising your child? Do they feel safe and empowered to express themselves? Do they see their home as a place of love and acceptance, or do they perceive it as a place where they must obey without question?

When children express feelings of being treated like slaves, it often indicates unresolved issues within the family that need attention. As a father, it's essential to recognize your mistakes and work on them in order to become a better person, a better Christian, and ultimately, a better parent. Ignoring your errors only leads to ignorance.

Strive to grow, change, and treat your children with the dignity they deserve. True love as a parent means wanting your children to thrive, not just giving them everything materially.

Love is about giving without expecting anything in return.
When you approach your child to ask for forgiveness, it's critical to avoid imposing any conditions. Instead, listen to them, offer a hug, and be there to provide advice if necessary. Avoid phrases like, "We need to talk because you did something wrong," as these can come off as judgmental and prideful.

Authentic reconciliation is built upon sincerity, honesty, repentance, love, and respect. You must be genuine in your apologies, as children can sense when an apology is insincere or just a formality.

Proverbs 3:3-4 states: "Never let loyalty or kindness abandon you! Tie them around your neck as a reminder. Write them deep in your heart. Then you will have both the favor of God and the people, and you will achieve a good reputation."

REMINDER:

- Never humiliate your child when asking for forgiveness.
- Don't force them to apologize; set the example by doing so first.
- Avoid punishing them after they have forgiven you.
- Once forgiveness is given, let it go; don't bring up past offenses.
- Let go of all resentment and pray for one another so that God's healing can be at work in your lives (James 5:16).
True healing comes through humility and grace, and it starts with the willingness to admit when we are wrong.

FREQUENTLY ASKED QUESTION:
How do I ask my son for forgiveness?
1. Pray for Guidance: Before approaching your child, take a moment to pray to God for wisdom and the strength needed for this important conversation.
2. Choose the Right Setting: Find a comfortable and private place to talk where you can resolve your differences without distractions.

3. Listen Actively: Approach the conversation without pre-judging your child. Take the time to truly listen to their feelings and perspectives.

Phase 3: ACTIONS, NOT WORDS

One of the greatest offenses a child can experience is hypocrisy from their parents. Children become frustrated and disillusioned when they see their parents preach one thing but live another. When parents teach values or principles they don't adhere to, it creates a moral, spiritual, and intellectual conflict that can severely damage family relationships.

Children are unlikely to believe what their parents preach until they see it enacted in real life. They may not obey until they observe consistent behavior that aligns with the lessons being taught. It's through observing your actions that your children truly understand and internalize the principles you're trying to impart.

The most important thing you can do for your children is to embody the values you preach. Don't preach what you don't practice. If there's room for improvement in your life, make that change! When God reveals something to you, it's meant to be lived out, not stored away.

Here are ways to demonstrate your love and commitment to your children:
- Show Love, Don't Just Say It: Instead of simply telling your children that you love them, find ways to demonstrate that love through your actions.
- Express Your Feelings: Instead of merely stating you missed them, make an effort to show it—spend quality time together and be present in their lives.
- Lead by Example: Rather than instructing your children to be better Christians, embody the values of your faith so they can see a living example to follow.
- Celebrate Their Achievements: Acknowledge their successes, birthdays, and milestones by investing your time and effort to

show that you care.
- Share Your Experiences: Don't just pass along religious teachings; convey your personal experiences and insights to nurture their growth.
In everything you do, focus on leading by example. Do you want your children to grow into better individuals? Take the necessary steps to invest in their lives—spend time with them, engage in their interests, and share your life lessons while also being open to learning from their experiences.
A united family, grounded in mutual respect and love, will stand strong against any adversity!

Chapter 11

Teach without Scolding

From a wise mind come wise words;
The words of the wise are persuasive.
Kind words are like honey: sweet for the soul
and healthy for the body.

Proverbs 16:23-24

yFrom a wise mind come good words;The words of the wise are Persuasive,kind words are like honey;sweet for the soul and healthy for the body

Proverbs 16:23-24(NLT)

The word art means: Capacity,ability to do something.
The word patience means:Ability to suffer or endure something without getting upset.

Each parent must learn to endure difficult situations without letting their emotions get the better of them. After the Crucifixion and Resurrection of Jesus, He spent 40 days with His disciples, imparting crucial teachings before ascending to heaven. One of His key messages, as stated in Acts 1:8, was: "But you will receive power when the Holy Spirit comes upon you; and you will be my witnesses and tell people about me everywhere: in Jerusalem, throughout Judea, in Samaria, and to the farthest places of the earth" (Acts 1:8, NLT).

The term "power" here encompasses the ability and capacity to act with purpose and conviction. For Christian parents, mastering the language of self-control and thoughtful communication is vital.

James' epistle to the church emphasizes the importance of self -control among believers, highlighting a significant gap in knowledge within the "Christian" community. Many within the church lack understanding, as there is a prevalent culture of ignorance. This includes individuals from various backgrounds —some educated and others who have navigated life without proper guidance.

In particular, the Latino culture has struggled with traditional disciplinary methods that often contradict biblical teachings. This cycle of unbiblical punishment and ineffective parenting must be addressed. As a parent, it's crucial to choose whether your children will be products of unchanging tradition or of transformative growth. In my experience, I hope my children will be shaped by transformation.

When rooted in tradition, families often carry wounds and limitations in their thinking. Conversely, being products of transformation encourages God to meet the individual needs of every family member. Today's younger generation tends to reject harmful traditions, understanding that these can lead to emotional damage rather than constructive growth.

As a parent, it is essential to recognize that in Christ, we no longer need to adhere to harmful family patterns, both in the household and with extended family. With our newfound knowledge, we have opportunities for growth and education in spiritual and familial matters.

The world is crying out for improved family education and alternative methods for raising children. Unfortunately, many still cling to outdated ideologies rooted in ignorance. It is up to us to break this cycle and recognize the damage caused by poor education for previous generations, which often leads to suffering, conflict, and loss.

We must not confine Jesus to the past; He is the same today and forever. God's mercy is abundant for anyone who seeks it and desires to change. This mercy extends not only to us as individuals but also to our children and their future generations. God offers vast and unlimited mercy, implying that our drive for knowledge and self-improvement should never wane. In God, there is no "stop" sign; He desires for each parent to diversify their knowledge and apply their learnings to raise the next generation equipped with understanding and wisdom.

Our children should be able to say, "I learned everything from my parents; they taught me all I needed to know." The world is filled with untapped potential—ideas, dreams, and wisdom— that went unshared due to the selfishness of those who withheld their knowledge.

Do not deprive your children of the valuable insights and lessons you have acquired. Throughout biblical history, we see examples of wise parents passing down their knowledge:

- Abraham shared his knowledge with Isaac.
- Isaac passed it on to Jacob.
- Jacob taught his twelve sons.
- Moses mentored Joshua.
- Elijah influenced Elisha.
- The priest Eli guided Samuel.
- Jesse imparted wisdom to David.
- David shared insights with Solomon.
- Joseph taught Jesus.

Every parent has a responsibility to share their experiences, knowledge, and the purpose they have discovered in life with their children. Failing to share this wisdom is tantamount to burying your legacy. A father who actively shares his story and experiences achieves a level of immortality through the lessons passed down to the next generation. Embrace this role, and ensure that your knowledge and love for learning enrich your children's lives for years to come.

FREQUENTLY ASKED QUESTION:

How can I teach my children what I know?

Answer:

How can I teach my children what I know?
The foundation of teaching your children involves consistent engagement from a young age. As stated in Deuteronomy 6:7-9 (KJV), "And you will repeat them to your children, and you will talk about them while you are in your house, when you walk along the road, and when you lie down, and when you get up. And you will bind them as a sign on your hand, and they will be as fronts between your eyes, and you will write them on the doorposts of your house and on your doors."

Additionally, Proverbs 3:3-4 (KJV) reminds us, "Let mercy and truth never depart from you; tie them around your neck, write them on the tablet of your heart; And you will find grace and good opinion in the eyes of God and men."

When teaching your children what you know, it is crucial to approach the process with mercy and patience. Even if they struggle to learn new concepts, you must encourage and support them, as this knowledge is often unfamiliar and requires time to absorb. This kind of teaching involves instilling key values and lessons that might not be formally taught in schools.

Your unique experiences and insights as a parent can greatly shape your children's lives. You hold the power to influence their legacy—whether they thrive and make a difference in the world or struggle without guidance.

Unfortunately, many parents fall into the trap of scolding their children, expecting them to learn proper behavior through punishment and harsh words. Instead, consider an alternative approach: What if we structured a learning plan?

A learning plan acts as a mental and spiritual framework that provides your children with a sense of purpose. Children are incredibly valuable and need direction from their parents to develop their potential over time. This plan can help facilitate effective and meaningful lessons, enabling them to understand and grow from their experiences.

How is a learning plan formed?

1. Chronological Development: Start the learning plan chronologically. Tailor your teachings based on your child's age and maturity. This ensures that the lessons are age-appropriate and resonates with their current understanding.
2. Diversified Teaching Methods: A good learning plan allows you to diversify your teaching methods and dynamics, ensuring that lessons adapt to your child's individual learning style. A prepared parent is like a soldier headed into battle—focused and ready to achieve their goals.

How can I start a learning plan?
- Identify Goals: Determine the type of children you want to

raise. What values or skills do you wish to instill in them?
- Recognize Obstacles: Understand the unique challenges each child faces. This awareness enables you to tailor your approach accordingly.

- Encourage Self-Discovery: Help each child explore questions such as, "What do you want in life?" or "What does God desire for you?" Assisting them in identifying their path is crucial for their development.

- Connect with God: Maintain a close relationship with God, seeking His guidance and insights regarding His plan for each of your children. Parenting centered on faith is essential, as God should be your source of wisdom and direction to lead your children on the right path.

By developing a structured learning plan infused with patience, understanding, and divine guidance, you can effectively equip your children with the knowledge and values they need to navigate life successfully.

FREQUENTLY ASKED QUESTION:

How should I teach my children without scolding?

Answer:
How should I teach my children without scolding?
To begin, let's clarify what scolding is: a reprimand or warning typically delivered with displeasure. When a parent scolds a child, it often conveys anger or discomfort aimed at prompting a change in behavior. However, understanding when and how to express concerns is crucial in nurturing your child's development.

Who Should Be Scolded?

It's essential to recognize that scolding should not be the go-to response for every situation. Children who lack understanding or instruction should never be scolded. If a child is innocent of wrongdoing or hasn't been adequately instructed on the correct behavior, reprimanding them only leads to insecurity and resentment.

Instead of scolding, if you find your child struggling to understand something, consider asking guiding questions such as:
- "Do you understand what I am asking of you?"
- "Are we on the same page?"
- "Could you repeat what I said to make sure you understood?"
- "Is there anything you don't understand that I can help clarify?"

The Impact of Angry Language

Many parents make the mistake of letting their anger dictate their responses, resulting in hurtful comments that can deeply affect a child's self-esteem. Phrases like:
- "Are you stupid?"
- "Why don't you understand, you fool?"
- "You are useless!"
- "You're worse than a donkey!"

All are detrimental to a child's emotional well-being. Such language is not only unfair but can also reflect poorly on the parent's character.

Throughout my experiences, I have encountered children from various backgrounds—some seemingly perfect on the outside—who suffer from emotional strain inflicted by harsh parenting. Children go through numerous daily challenges, and when they are met with negative reinforcement from their parents, it becomes difficult for them to practice the lessons they've learned at home.

The Importance of Self-Reflection

Parents must also be aware of their own behavior and the vocabulary they use. Accepting responsibility for inappropriate actions is crucial. Acknowledging when a reaction was unjust

or excessive allows for healing between parent and child.
It's important to understand that pointing fingers and assigning blame only complicates matters. If a child doesn't comply or understand, it doesn't justify hurtful words or actions. As parents, you are called to reflect God's love and understanding, treating your children with compassion.

Biblical Guidance

The Bible offers clear guidance in Ephesians 6:4 (NLT): "Parents, don't make your children angry by the way you treat them. Rather, bring them up with the discipline and instruction that comes from the Lord."

Steps for Instructing and Correcting without Scolding

1. **Avoid Angering Your Child:** Reflect on whether your actions or words are causing unnecessary anger or hurt. Understand that your children have feelings and emotions that can be easily harmed.

2. **Recognize Their Perspective:** Understand that children are navigating their own challenges. Just like adults, they may struggle with understanding the teaching or expectations set before them.

3. **Live the Principles You Teach:** Children are more likely to embrace values and principles when they see them modeled in their parents' lives. If parents preach values but do not live by them, children may grow disinterested or resistant.

4. **Practice Compassionate Communication:** Foster an environment of understanding and patience. Approach teaching with love, and engage in constructive dialogue that encourages growth and reflection.

By implementing these steps, you can create a nurturing environment that promotes learning and understanding while avoiding the pitfalls of scolding. Your goal should be to raise confident, emotionally secure children who feel loved and understood, allowing them to thrive and develop into their best selves.

FREQUENTLY ASKED QUESTION:

How can I avoid problems between my children and me?

Answer:

1. Never disrespect him when you are angry.
2. Never underdo it.
3. Never describe it.
4. Never use the phrase: "I am your father" to justify your bad actions, bad behavior, or rude words and actions. Assume the truths they tell you, take responsibility, and change as a human being—this is what the Bible teaches us!

Talk to him as if he were a human being that you are meeting for the first time. Never be fooled into thinking that just because he is your child, he gives you the right to harm him with words and actions. God lent you your children so that you could enjoy them and raise them in their knowledge, not so that you could destroy them with hurtful words and actions.

Remember: He who hurts a son is a friend of the devil; he who raises a son is a friend of God.

"The purpose of the thief is to steal and kill and destroy;my purpose is to give you a full and abundant life(John 10:10 NLT).

Raise him in discipline, that is, teach him the habits that he must know how to exercise and put into practice. It is unfair and wrong when a father (or mother) wants to correct a child for something that he or she was not taught. A father who tries hard and puts in enough effort and dedication, teaching everything a child should know, has the right and respect of his children when there is a mistake.

Otherwise, children who are not raised with habits and

customs are difficult to teach and change when they grow up. Instruct them with knowledge that comes from God. What does this mean? This means that the Word of God must come first before any personal thoughts that may interfere with parenting. You cannot instruct a child with human knowledge, because human knowledge is limited and perverse. But the Word of God is living, effective, and sharper than a two-edged sword.

FREQUENTLY ASKED QUESTION:
How should you scold?

Answer:

"From a wise mind come good words;The words of the wise are persuasive,Kind words are like honey;"sweet for the soul and healthy for the body."(Proverbs 16:23-24 NLT).

For many years and centuries, we have heard of parents who scold their children with hurtful words and painful actions that destroy the heart and emotions, but no one thinks about how they should scold their children. The main thing a parent must understand is that a scolding is a correction, not an upset moment of yelling, hitting, and touching. When a parent is about to scold, they should take the time and use the right words to correct the child appropriately so that he:

- Understands what he did wrong.
- Corrects his mistake.
- Makes the effort to do better.
- Can become a better person.

A scolding should never be carried out with violence and hurtful words; this is called "abuse or domestic violence." Correcting a child means helping him understand that he did wrong, that he did not do it well, or that he is doing it incorrectly. For this, there must be an exchange of words with serenity and wisdom. A father must understand that when he corrects, it is because he is about to share wisdom, experience, and knowledge, not the other way around.

Many believe that the correct way to scold and draw attention to children is to demonstrate fury and displeasure. However, this only creates embarrassing scenes and brings resentment to both parties. A father must be wise and astute when correcting and always remember that before anger comes serenity, patience, mercy, and unconditional love for his children. Children are not raised with shouting and violence; they are raised with love and mercy.

FREQUENTLY ASKED QUESTION:

How can I address my children appropriately,politely and wisely?

Answer:

There are three scenes that always appear in parents' anger when their children make a mistake or inconvenience: in public, at home, and when they're out of reach. A parent must know how to control the situation without letting things get out of hand. Everything must be done with control and wisdom. This means that a parent should try not to expose the disciplinary intimacy of the family. Parents should never call out their children in front of the public or when they are out of reach.

A father must be wise when it comes to getting his children's attention. What is recommended for parents and the entire family to avoid embarrassment and uncomfortable moments is to have a strategic plan that can control the situation without making a fuss. This means they should have plans A, B, and C for when they face an uncomfortable moment. In this way, they can avoid embarrassment and uncomfortable situations, maintaining the family's posture before others.

FREQUENTLY ASKED QUESTION:

What is plan A,B,C?

Answer:

Children in general have similar behaviors, which include irritation, disobedience, and ignorance. Plans A, B, and C must be ready so that when the moment arises, parents will not have to struggle or face difficulty in deciding, "What do we do?" in the middle of an awkward moment.

The strategic plan consists of predetermined decisions so that it can be executed easily and effectively within the three common areas of concern. This helps parents avoid making people around them uncomfortable and prevents others from having to make their own separate plans or leave because of what is happening.

FREQUENTLY ASKED QUESTION:

What examples are there to carry out plan A,B,C?

Answer:

These are some examples so you can decide what to do in an uncomfortable moment.

Example 1:A child is crying and throwing a tantrum because he wants candy or a toy. His frustration stems from not being able to have what he desires at that moment.

Plan A: Scold him and tell him no
Plan B: Hit him and tell him no
Plan C: Let him cry and make others uncomfortable
Plan D: Leave the place and return another time

Which plan do you think would be correct?
The correct plan for such a situation is Plan A,and Plan D

Explanation: A parent must end the situation as soon as possible by covering 3 things.
1)	The comfort of those around you

2) Teaching the child to understand that it cannot be done at the moment.
3) Avoid embarrassment, having everyone stare at you for how your child behaves.

Bonus: If the child understands,explain the reason for your answer.

Example#2: A teenager is crying and throwing a tantrum because he wants to go out and play with his friends.

Plan A: Scold him and tell him no
Plan B: Hit him and tell him no
Plan C: Let him cry and make others uncomfortable
Plan D: Sit down and explain why he can't go

Which plan do you think would be correct?
The correct plan for such a situation is Plan A and Plan D

Explanation: A parent with a teenager must exercise patience and dedicate time to provide essential knowledge and guidance. It's crucial for teens to understand: "How are decisions made?" "Why should a particular decision be made?" "What benefits come from that decision?" and "How can one change a decision?"

Teenagers often experience shifts in their perspectives, hormones, and thoughts as they grow and absorb information. A responsible parent takes the time to explain, guide, and warn them about potential consequences of their actions. This approach not only helps the teenager understand various situations but also equips them with knowledge and experience, teaching them how to earn privileges responsibly.

Example#3: A young man is throwing a tantrum on the phone because he wants to go out with his friends for a walk. In his frustration, he resorts to insulting and getting angry, even breaking his cell phone. However, he doesn't have permission to go out because his behavior has been inappropriate, and he hasn't been responsible with his chores around the house.

Plan A: Say no
Plan B: Yell at him on the phone
Plan C: Go get him to take him home
Plan D: Persuade him to go home
Plan E: Talk to your friends to find out where they are going

Which plan do you think would be correct?

The correct plan for such a situation is Plan A,Plan C and Plan D

Explanation: A parent should never leave his children in the care of other parents' children, especially if he doesn't know them well. The priority should always be to care for, protect, guide, and educate children. The risk of them being influenced by negative behaviors or facing emotional and psychological harm increases significantly when parents are absent and place too much trust in children who are not yet mature enough to make sound decisions.

As this chapter illustrates, scolding does not mean resorting to violence or harsh punishment. Instead, scolding, disciplining, or correcting should focus on helping a child understand: what is good or bad, what actions are correct, what mistakes they made, and what behaviors to avoid. It's also about teaching them what can be prevented by following guidance and the benefits of adhering to instructions.

Before reacting out of frustration, parents should ask themselves several questions: Why did my child behave this way? What motivated their choices? What factors contributed to their actions? How can I help my child gain a better understanding of the situation? Is there something I might learn from my child's perspective?

It's crucial to think critically before taking action. Analyze the consequences of your decisions. Before scolding, take the time to reflect. Prior to resorting to physical discipline, consider if it is truly necessary and how to communicate your message effectively. Assess the seriousness of the situation before deciding on a corrective approach.

ESSENTIAL NOTES

The most important step before any form of correction is to take a moment to lay your hands on your child and pray for God to grant them wisdom, peace, and understanding. It's essential to remain calm and confident, trusting that God will work within them.

Additionally, it is important to discern the right approach to take in each situation. By maintaining this spiritual connection and sense of calmness, parents can create an environment that encourages growth and understanding, rather than fear or resentment. This foundation of love and guidance is vital for fostering a positive relationship between parent and child.

REMEMBER:

"From a wise mind come good words;The words of the wise are persuasive,kind words are like honey;sweet to the soul and healthy for the body"(Proverbs 16:23-24 NLT)

Those who have understanding do not lose their temper;Those who are easily angered demonstrate great foolishness

(Proverbs 14:29 NLT).

Chapter 12

Family Culture

Children are a gift from the Lord, they are a reward from Him. Children born to a young man are like arrows in the hands of a warrior. How happy is the man who has his quiver full of them! He will not be ashamed when he faces his accusers at the city gates.

Psalms 127:3-5

FAMILY DAY

Behold,children are an inheritance from the Lord;The fruit of the womb is a thing of esteem.Like arrows in the hand of a brave man,so are the children born in youth.Blessed is the man who filled his quiver with them;He will not be put to shame when he speaks to enemies at the gate(Psalms 127:3-5 KJV).

We have all heard, or at least have an idea of what family day is like in a church. Usually, when a pastor mentions that such a day is family day, he always refers to it as a time for quality moments with children and couples—an opportunity to nurture attention, chemistry, and love within the family. This day is intended to be special, where parents and children put aside their usual activities to focus on talking, playing, eating, and enjoying time together. Typically, by tradition, pastors fill the week with various activities designed to promote the leadership and spiritual growth of all church members: men, women, youth, adolescents, and children.

As a pastor's son and a member of various churches in the past, I've had the blessing of being aware of my surroundings from an early age. Growing up within the church, I've had the chance to develop in every area and experience various perspectives. From Sunday school to leadership meetings with ministers, deacons, youth, and children, I've seen what church life is like from different angles. This in-person experience has helped me identify areas needing attention or those that require more independence and practical involvement. The church truly is a puzzle without limits, with always something new to learn, experiment with, and develop. And at its core, the family is the heartbeat of the church.

In my role as a minister and as a pastor's son, I've noticed a significant void in church activities. While there are frequent events, conferences, and trainings, there seems to be a glaring absence of parent training or family restoration services. This oversight is concerning. In our congregations, children serve as the material that bonds relationships within the church. Virtually everyone with a family in the church has children, which means it's something we all share and identify with as a community.

Yet, the challenges faced by children in the church are serious:
- Rebellion
- Straying from faith
- Disconnect from God
- Emotional trauma
- Confusion
- Lack of attention
- Absence of discipline
- Lack of love

This list often seems repetitive, leading to a cycle that continues within the church due to a deficit of discernment, attention, maturity, experience, and divine direction. It's crucial to recognize that children are not just here to make parents happy or be part of a loving family; they will ultimately grow up, make their own choices, and have families of their own.

In our current climate, there appears to be a trend focused solely on adult needs, often neglecting the developmental needs of children. Parents need to realize that children don't wait until they're ten years old to start understanding the world around them. Their mental, emotional, and spiritual development heavily depends on the activities and atmosphere they find themselves in.

The scriptures remind us to "pray and be vigilant because the enemy walks like a roaring lion." This indicates that the enemy waits for moments of neglect to instill confusion, hatred, and resentment, which can lead to anxiety, depression, and various emotional issues in children.

Often, parents approach pastors in hopes of guidance for their children, but there are limitations to what a pastor can accomplish in these situations. It is ultimately the parents' responsibility to advise, correct, direct, and discipline their children. While children may benefit from a pastor's words of wisdom, it is the parents who provide the ongoing motivation and encouragement.

Even if a child spends all day with a pastor, learning, it is still the parents' role to ensure that those teachings translate into daily life. Parents are the foremost role models for their children. No one influences a child more than their parents. If parents exhibit poor behavior, the likelihood is high that their children will mirror that. Conversely, if parents demonstrate wisdom and good values, they're instilling the same in their children. Each child is shaped under the guidance of their parents.

FREQUENTLY ASKED QUESTION:

What can I do to take time with my children and solve the personal problems they encounter?

Answer:
To gain a clearer understanding of your children and the challenges they face, it's essential to get closer to them and foster transparency within the family. Building that connection creates a safe space for open communication and trust.

This family circle guide can assist you in putting these principles into practice, allowing you to nurture closeness and take responsibility for your children's wellbeing. By doing so, you will strengthen the love and bonds of brotherhood in the family, creating a healthier and more supportive home environment.

Here are some steps to help you get started:
1. Regular Family Meetings: Set aside time each week for family discussions. This provides an opportunity for everyone to share their feelings, thoughts, and concerns in a structured environment.
2. Active Listening: Make a conscious effort to listen to your children without interrupting. Validate their feelings and encourage them to express themselves openly.

3. Shared Activities: Engage in activities that everyone enjoys, whether it's playing games, cooking together, or going for walks. These moments of fun can strengthen connections and create lasting memories.
4. Open Communication: Encourage honesty by being open yourself. Share your experiences and feelings to let your children know that it's okay to be vulnerable.

5. Set Family Goals: Work together to establish goals as a family, whether they are related to education, hobbies, or even simple household chores. This promotes teamwork and a sense of belonging.

6. Create a Safe Space: Ensure your home is a safe haven where children can express themselves without fear of judgment or punishment. This encourages them to be candid about their struggles.

7. Make Time for One-on-One: Spend individual time with each child. This helps them feel special and valued, making it easier for them to open up about personal issues.

By consistently applying these practices, you'll foster a closer, more trustworthy relationship with your children and create an environment where love and brotherhood can thrive.

FAMILY CIRCLE GUIDE

PURPOSES: CLOSER TO GOD AND THE FAMILY
ACTIVITY: The family must choose an activity to live together and have a good time. During the activity, they can have food and/or snacks to foster togetherness and unity. This can take place at home or away from home.

FOOD: The focal point is family; therefore, they can choose what they want, as there are no limits. A family circle serves to promote connection and conversation.

PRAYER: The family should start this gathering with a prayer, thanking God for the food and for allowing everyone to be present. Both parents and children should share a quick prayer, asking God for guidance and wisdom to grow as a family and fulfill the purpose He has for each member in their lives.

THANKSGIVING: After each recognition, it's important to applaud and celebrate one another for achievements and goals accomplished. Parents will start by acknowledging each other's efforts during the week in front of the children, encouraging the kids to express gratitude for their parents, appreciating their hard work. Following this, parents will recognize and thank their children for their accomplishments, whether academic, personal, or general. Siblings should also take a moment to celebrate each other's individual, family, and household successes.

FAMILY GOALS: Parents need to decide and set long-term, monthly, and weekly family goals so that children understand the family's purpose and direction.

FAMILY PROBLEMS: Parents should inform their children about current family issues, including economic costs such as utilities, food, gas, and rent. This promotes maturity, consideration, and inclusion among the children.

INTRA-FAMILY PROBLEMS: The family should discuss any ongoing issues. This is an ideal time for parents to address conflicts between siblings or to apologize to each other for previous mistakes made in front of the children.

INDIVIDUAL PROBLEMS: Parents will freely ask their children about their personal situations and discuss any insecurities, worries, stagnations, or personal battles. NOTE: Before starting this conversation, ensure that children understand that everyone's voice is valid. Mockery, contempt, or judgment should not occur; everyone must show mercy before speaking or suggesting anything.

INTRA-FAMILY COUNSELING: After listening to their children's insecurities and personal problems, parents should reassure them of their worth and capabilities. They can offer guidance that helps children understand life's purpose, acknowledging the reasons behind their experiences, especially in relation to God's plan for their lives. Encourage constructive advice among siblings to build confidence and knowledge.

TROUBLESHOOTING: Parents need to communicate observations made during the week regarding poor behavior, irresponsibility, low grades, disrespect, or lack of education. They should ask their children why they acted as they did, explain why it was inappropriate, and teach how to approach the situation correctly and the reasoning behind it.

INTRA-FAMILY FORGIVENESS: Parents should emphasize the importance of apologies. They can start by acknowledging their own mistakes that may have offended their children. Everyone should be willing to put pride aside to apologize for the sake of harmony and coexistence in the family.

CHILDREN COUNSELING: Parents should take time to ask their children questions such as:
- How could they be better for their kids?
- What do they need to work on as parents?
- What don't the children like about them?
- What complaints do the children have?
- What did they fail at during the week?
- What changes would the children like to see from their parents?

PARENT: Parents should document their children's suggestions and complaints in a notebook to address these issues and improve.

TEACHING OF THE WEEK: Parents should share a lesson learned or an experience from the week that could be beneficial for their children. The goal is to impart wisdom and

knowledge gained through experience.
Read Deuteronomy 6:4-9

QUICK PRAYER: Parents and children should say a prayer together, thanking God for helping them understand their family situation, for His guidance in solving problems, and for the spiritual, emotional, and physical healing and liberation He brings into their lives. They can ask for God's protection and blessings as they go about their days, wherever they may walk. This is also a time to bless the children, showing them love and brotherly affection, as well as encouraging the children to express their love toward their parents.

Always remember:
The purpose of this activity is for the family to:
- Be transparent
- Resolve differences
- Forgive each other
- Address doubts and complaints
Above all, remember that God and family come first.

———

Chapter 13

Fists to Swords

If someone says: "I love God", but hates another believer, that person is a liar because, if we do not love those whom we can see, how can we love God, whom we cannot see?

1 John 4:20

If someone says:"I love God",but hates another believer,that person is a liar because,if we do not love those whom we can see,how can we love God,whom we cannot see?

(1 John 4:20 NLT)

The book of principles is filled with fascinating stories that act as a mirror, reflecting our own lives and families. Within its pages, we find the accounts of Adam, Noah, Abraham, Isaac, Jacob, and their families. These patriarchs served as vessels through which God consistently demonstrated His mercy, allowing us to observe the varied lifestyles and unique experiences each had with God.

Despite being family descendants, Noah, Abraham, Isaac, and Jacob each had distinct experiences. Abraham was known as the friend of God, Isaac represented the fulfillment of promise, and Jacob was the father of the twelve tribes of Israel, through whom the remnant and the Savior would arise.

Before the narrative unfolds, Jacob faced struggles in his life, particularly concerning the wife he loved deeply, Rachel. Jacob had a tumultuous history, marked by betrayal and conflict. His love for Rachel was profound; the moment he first laid eyes on her, he was so moved that he wept. Determined, he worked for fourteen years to win her affection.

However, Jacob encountered a significant hurdle—Rachel could not bear children. After years of longing, Rachel urged Jacob to have children with her servant, seeking fulfillment through others, yet her heart remained empty. Eventually, God showed mercy and allowed Rachel to conceive, giving birth to her first son, Joseph.

Joseph's life was anything but ordinary; he faced immense challenges from his early years to adulthood. His brothers' envy of Joseph's special status in Jacob's eyes led them to plot against him, resulting in emotional detachment from their father. Joseph's understanding of his father's love for him contrasted sharply with his brothers' jealousy, which had festered for years.

This serves as a critical lesson for parents: dysfunctional families do not emerge overnight; they are often cultivated through ongoing neglect of behavioral red flags. Each small offense, if ignored, builds up over time, weakening familial bonds. Parents should be vigilant and correct harmful behaviors immediately. The jealousy Joseph's brothers harbored did not manifest overnight; rather, it simmered and grew for 17 years. If Jacob had recognized the need for balanced love among his children, perhaps he could have mitigated Joseph's suffering.

God's mercy is profound, turning human errors into divine purposes. If your child is struggling emotionally or spiritually, understand that mistakes can be transformed into lessons about life, reconciliation, and healing. It's never too late for children to reform; they can be guided back to becoming good individuals, and your past mistakes can still be remedied. Place your concerns in God's hands; He will guide you through your children's wisdom to foster healing.

God desires for you to repair the damage you've caused within your family. Acknowledge your shortcomings as a parent, teacher, and guide. If you've faced ongoing struggles with your children, remember that they reflect the consequences of earlier mistakes born from anger, carelessness, or poor decisions.

2 Corinthians 9:6 reminds us: "He who sows sparingly will also reap sparingly; and he who sows generously will also reap generously." Understand that your children may have been deprived of love and nurturing for too long, which can lead to harmful behaviors. Change must start with you; stop the cycle of negativity before it consumes your family.

Ask yourself:
- Do I want my family to crumble?
- What do I desire for my family?
- Where is our family headed?

It's time to end the fighting! Stop handing your children to negativity and destruction through irresponsibility and resentment. Recognize that your true enemy is not each other —it is the destructive influences pervasive in society.

God is looking for warriors who will combat evil and societal pressures, not for fighters within their own families. Divert your focus to God and commit to fighting for your children's well-being.

Gaining worldly success means nothing if your family is lost. Cease the arguments and unnecessary conflicts. Stop allowing negativity to poison your relationships. Your first adversary is often within yourself.

A preacher's power comes from living a life imbued with the Word of God. Let the Scriptures fill your heart and guide your actions. Exchange your physical struggles for the spiritual sword that combats evil. Equip yourself to protect your family with the truth of God's Word and strive for the peace and harmony that God intends for your household.

Transform your hands—use them to uplift, heal, and encourage your loved ones. Trade your fists for the love, truth, and harmony that will nurture growth in your family and foster an environment where all can thrive.

Testimony

Daniel Becerra grew up in a family that seemed to have it all but, over time, became completely dysfunctional. He believed that the collapse of his family also meant the end of his ministry, his calling, his legacy, and everything he had worked hard for since childhood. Relationships with his parents and brothers were fraught with conflict, and one day, Daniel simply grew tired of fighting over trivial matters.

Determined to change the narrative, Daniel resolved to be

different and to help other families in similar situations. He made a conscious decision that his family's failures would not dictate his future or his ability to serve God. With a renewed sense of purpose, he recognized that as long as he had life, health, and faith in God, he could break the generational curse of mediocrity and never standing out that had plagued his family.

Daniel dedicated himself to helping young people, pastors, ministers, and anyone in need of God's love and guidance. His journey serves as a testament that if a young person from a dysfunctional family can make a meaningful impact on countless lives, then anyone can change the course of their family's history.

You too can take the leap and change your family's trajectory. Don't allow yourself to get stuck! Fight against the odds and battle through the challenges you face. With perseverance and faith, you will overcome. In the name of Jesus, believe that your family can be transformed and blessed by the blood of the one who sacrificed everything for our mercy and eternal love, offered to us by our heavenly Father every day of our lives.

Beloved,I wish that you may prosper in all things,and that you may be in health,just as your soul prospers.(3 John 1:2 KJV).

NOTES

Chapter 1
https://dle.rae.es/exasper ar Chapter3
https://cimacnoticias.com.mx/noticia/fracasa-la-education-sexual-en-méxico-revela-encuesta/
Chapter 6
https://www.mhanational.org/list-verification-of-the-signs-of-depression

https://www.healthline.com/health/es/symptoms
-of-anxiety#2.-Feelings-of-agitation
https://ifightdepression.com/es/for-all/signs-and-symptoms
Chapter 7
Chapter 8
https://dle.rae.es/arte
https://dle.rae.es/paciencia?m=form
https://dle.rae.es/poder?m=form
https://www.biblegateway.com/passage/?search=Acts
+1&See if
https://www.biblegateway.com/passage/?search=Santiago
%203&version=NTVon=NTV
https://frasesbuenas.net/lo-que-alimentas-dentro/
https://www.biblegateway.com/passage/?search=Romans
+12&version=NTV
https://www.biblegateway.com/passage/?search=Galatas+5&ve
rsion=NTV
https://www.biblegateway.com/passage/?search=Mateo+1
6%3 A24&version=NTV
https://espanol.womenshealth.gov/relationships-and-
safety/domestic-violence/effects-domestic-violence-
children(The materials on these pages are not restricted by
copyright and may be copied,reproduced or duplicated without
permission from the Office on Women's Health at the US
Department of Health and Human Services)
Chapter 9
https://definiciona.com/productivo/http://etimologias.dechile.net/?pr
oductivo
Chapter 11
https://definicion.de/regano/https://www.biblegateway.com/passa
g e/?search=Psalms+127&version=RVR1960
Chapter 12
https://www.biblegateway.com/passage/?search=Psalms+127&versi
on=RVR1960
Chapter 13
1 John 4:20(NLT)

Bibliography

Google.com   cimacnoticias.com.mx   rae.es(Royal   Spanish
Academy)
www.biblegateway.comwww.mhanational.orgwww.healthline.comifig
htdepression.comphrasesbuenas.net
espanol.womenshealth.gov

ABOUT THE AUTHOR

Daniel J. Becerra is a public speaker, psalmist, pastor, and composer with a deep passion for seeing souls transformed through the message of Jesus. Growing up in the gospel, he has devoted his life to ministry, serving in various roles within the church, including youth leader, worship leader, and supervisor of leadership in the churches he has helped build alongside his father.

His extensive ministry experience has allowed him to cultivate meaningful relationships with notable authors and speakers in the field, all committed to being part of a new revival within the church. Daniel's dedication is focused on saving souls, restoring families, and inspiring a new generation to rise and fulfill their calling in faith.

He carries a particular burden for the youth and children of pastors who have faced hurt and longing for change in their lives. His greatest desire is to be an instrument of God, guiding those who have strayed back to the path of peace and salvation, helping them reconnect with God's love and purpose.

Email: **becerradaniel22@gmail.com**
Facebook and Instagram: Daniel J.Becerra